CW00997016

Contents

Unit 1

1   Read the letter and try to explain the idioms in bold.

Dear Mary,

Sorry Lionel and I were such poor company last weekend, but we were both feeling **1) down in the dumps,** especially after finding out that Terry had been **2) keeping us in the dark** about the severity of the company's money problems. I was so angry with him. My own brother — can you believe it? Believe me, running a family business **3) isn't all it's cracked up to be!**

Anyway, the morning after you left, I was reading the paper when an advert for a week in a country cottage **4) caught my eye.** It sounded **5) right up our street,** so I mentioned it to Lionel and, after a lot of persuading, he finally agreed that we both needed to **6) take things easy** for a bit.

We've been here for five days now and I feel so much better. It's right **7) off the beaten track,** so Lionel and I have had enough peace and quiet to talk about the company's problems and come up with some solutions. I'll tell you one thing — Terry is going to **8) come down to earth with a bump** when we get back!

This place is truly fantastic, and Lionel's **9) in his element** at the moment as the river near here is excellent for fishing. He got up at **10) the crack of dawn** today and returned at lunch-time with an enormous trout!

I'd better go now as we're leaving tomorrow and I haven't started packing yet. I'll give you a ring as soon as we get back.

Love,
Jane

2   Match the items with the idioms from Ex. 1.

a	to relax	f	within one's range of interests/ knowledge
b	to keep sb unaware of sth	g	depressed
c	to be not as good as people say	h	very happy/suited to a situation
d	to stop dreaming and start thinking practically	i	to get sb's attention
e	isolated and quiet	j	very early in the morning

3   Fill in the gaps with phrases from the list:

kept in the dark, caught my eye, down in the dumps, came down to earth with a bump, all it's cracked up to be

1   Sam thought he could pass his exam without studying, but he .... when he failed.
2   He was .... about his surprise retirement party.
3   The new restaurant isn't ....; it may look nice, but the food is awful!
4   I bought Ann some flowers because she looked ....
5   The beautiful clothes in the shop window ...., so I went in and bought a dress.

4   Fill in the gaps with phrases from the list:

right up my street, take things easy, the crack of dawn, off the beaten track, in your element

Greg: Hi Jim. How did you spend your week off?
Jim: I went camping in Snowdonia. It was brilliant; no phones or traffic or anything like that for a whole week. It was completely **1)** ....
Greg: That sounds **2)** ....! I could do with a few days out of the city.
Jim: Yeah. Imagine it Greg — getting up at **3)** .... every day and watching the sun rise as you cook your breakfast, then a bit of walking or fishing with no one telling you what to do.
Greg: You must have been **4)** ...., Jim.
Jim: You're right there! Actually, I'm going again next weekend. Do you want to come?
Greg: Maybe another time. I think I'll just stay at home and **5)** .... instead.

5 Read the advertisement and try to explain the idioms in bold.

1) GET AWAY FROM IT ALL

ON THE COSTA BLANCA

Hotel Blanca

- *1 week - only £100*
- *5-star hotel, full board*
- *lively holiday resort*

Phone: 01215 49268

Tired of holidaying in the same old **2) run-of-the-mill** places? Are you searching for sandy white beaches where you can sunbathe till you're **3) as brown as a berry**, or **4) round-the-clock** bars and discos where you can dance all night? If so, then **5) your best bet** is the Costa Blanca in Spain.

You'll be **6) over the moon** with both the Hotel Blanca and its delightful location on the Spanish coast, where you'll find a multitude of ways to **7) get into the swing of** your holiday, ranging from jet-skiing to paragliding. Food-lovers won't be disappointed either, as the Hotel Blanca has two terrific restaurants. One word of warning, however, for more conventional diners — **8) steer clear** of the *Chili a la Blanca* — it's hot!

So, if you fancy a holiday where you can **9) let your hair down**, and return home with **10) a new lease of life** — try the Hotel Blanca — we guarantee you won't regret it.

6 Match the items with the idioms from Ex. 5.

a	to take a break from work or problems	**f**	all day and all night
b	a return of energy or enthusiasm	**g**	to become accustomed to sth and start enjoying it
c	to relax and enjoy oneself	**h**	to avoid (sb/sth)
d	extremely pleased	**i**	very suntanned
e	the most appropriate choice	**j**	ordinary and un-exciting

7 Rewrite the following sentences using the words in bold. Do not change these words in any way.

1 Speaking in front of an audience can be nerve-racking, but once you become accustomed to it, you'll find it easy.
swing ....

2 My apartment block has a 24-hour security system.
clock ....

3 I'm tired of ordinary novels. I want to read something original.
mill ....

4 We decided to go to a desert island so that we could escape from our daily problems.
away ....

5 I was extremely happy when I won first prize.
moon ....

8 Replace the words in bold with phrases from the list.

steer clear of, letting my hair down, new lease of life, best bet, was as brown as a berry

On the first day of my summer holiday in France I was in the mood for **enjoying myself and having some fun,** and finally I decided that a day of jet-skiing would be **my most suitable option.** Once I had learnt how to control the machine and **stay away from** the big waves, I really started to enjoy whizzing across the surface of the sea. When I arrived back at the hotel I **had a fantastic suntan** and felt as if I had been given a **burst of new energy.** It was a great way to start my holiday.

9 **Fill in the gaps with phrases from the list:**

down in the dumps   *take things easy*   *caught my eye*
best bet   *a new lease of life*   *run-of-the-mill*
right up your street   *let our hair down*
get away from it all   *off the beaten track*

1 The doctor told him to .... until he was strong enough to work again.
2 Sharon felt ...., so we decided to try and cheer her up.
3 This interesting magazine article ...., so I decided to send it to you.
4 This beach is .... so very few people know about it.
5 Grandpa seems so much happier since his retirement; it's given him ....
6 If you're looking for a cheap holiday, your .... is Wright's Travel.
7 After a tense week at work, we decided to go out on Friday night and ....
8 This resort is a bit ....; it has some good points, but it's nothing special.
9 I think you'll find this restaurant is ....; it's got great food, it's quiet and very reasonable.
10 The politician needed a break from his busy schedule, so he went on a sailing trip to ....

....

10 **Rewrite the following sentences using the words in bold. Do not change these words in any way.**

1 This novel isn't as good as everyone says it is.
cracked ....
2 I play badminton quite often now that I know the game and I'm getting better at it.
swing ....
3 After her holiday, trouble at work made Martha face reality again.
earth ....
4 Janet was really happy at the disco as she loves dancing.
element ....
5 It's the first time we've won the cup and we're delighted.
moon ....
6 John worked all day and all night to finish the assignment.
clock ....
7 Since shellfish upsets my stomach, I try to avoid it.
steer ....
8 My father didn't tell me about my mother's illness.
dark ....

9 After a week on the beach in Tunisia, I have a great suntan.
berry ....
10 I get up early in order to avoid the traffic on the way to work.
crack ....

11 **Answer the questions below:**

1 Can something be **off the beaten track** and **right up your street** at the same time? Why/Why not?
2 If you **came down to earth with a bump**, would you be **in your element**? Why/Why not?
3 If you discovered that the hotel where you were staying **wasn't all it was cracked up to be**, would you get up at **the crack of dawn** and leave? Why/Why not?

12 **Use the words missing from the sentences below to complete the crossword.**

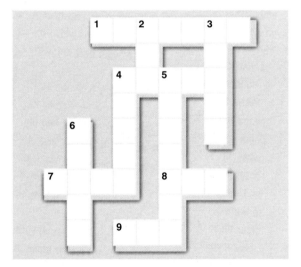

Across

1 This hotel isn't all it's .... up to be.
4 The Star Hotel is awful — steer .... of it.
7 She kept her parents in the .... about her new boyfriend.
8 This vase caught my .... at the antique shop.
9 I think the African safari would be your best .... for a holiday.

Down

2 I should take a holiday; I need to get away from it .... .
3 He'll come down to .... with a bump when he finds out the truth.
4 You can get a snack anytime as the coffee bar is open round the ....
5 Dave loves gardening; he's in his .... when he's outdoors.
6 The house is difficult to find as it's off the beaten ....

1 Read the letter and try to explain the idioms in bold.

Dear Mum,

Just a quick note to ask you for a bit of advice. I'm quite worried about Sharon and I just don't know what to do.

She came round a few weeks ago to tell me that she'd been on a date with Paul Regan, **1) an old flame** of hers from university. Now, I don't know if you remember him, but I do — he **2) stole her heart** at the beginning of her first year and she was convinced that she'd met **3) the man of her dreams**. For a while it seemed that he was **4) head over heels in love** with her too, but then, all of a sudden, at the end of her second year, he told her he never wanted to see her again and **5) broke her heart**.

Anyway, it seems that he's had **6) a change of heart**, but I just don't trust him. She says she's not interested in him, but quite obviously she is. She can't hide the way she feels — you know how she **7) wears her heart on her sleeve**. I know Sharon and I haven't always **8) seen eye to eye** on a lot of matters, but she is my sister and I do care about her. What worries me is that the same thing might happen again.

I know **9) all's fair in love and war**, but as I said, I don't want to watch her go through it all over again. Could you talk to her, please?

Love,
Brenda

P.S. Mum, careful what you tell her because right now, she thinks Paul **10) is the bee's knees.**

2 Match the items with the idioms from Ex. 1.

a	a change of one's feelings for sth/sb	**g**	to make sb fall in love with one
b	to allow one's feelings to be too obvious	**h**	to be the best there is
c	very much in love with sb	**i**	to agree (about matters)
d	sb one was once in love with	**j**	all actions are justified when there are feelings of love/rivalry
e	the ideal man		
f	to cause sb great unhappiness		

3 Fill in the gaps with phrases from the list:

head over heels in love, a change of heart, broke his heart, bee's knees, see eye to eye

1 Sally .... when she told John she was leaving him.
2 David must have had .... because he's decided to move to Manchester after all.
3 Tracy thinks her new boyfriend is the .... — she never stops talking about him.
4 After their first date they fell .... with each other.
5 Robert and I are always arguing — we never .... on anything.

4 Fill in the gaps with phrases from the list:

the man of her dreams, wear your heart on your sleeve, an old flame, stole your heart, all's fair in love and war

Frank: Hi, Mike. I ran into **1)** .... of yours yesterday.
Mike: Oh, really! Who?
Frank: Karen, of course. The one who **2)**............ .... on that holiday in Andorra.
Mike: Of course, Karen. How is she?
Frank: Fine. She's getting married next year.
Mike: Hmm. She said I was **3)** .... in Andorra. I really loved her, you know.
Frank: I know she betrayed you, Mike. But then, as they say, "**4)** .... ". Next time, don't **5)** ....

5 Read the dialogue and try to explain the idioms in bold. Then look at the picture and say which idiom it represents.

Gladys: Morning Mabel. You'll never guess who I got a letter from today!

Mabel: Go on, who?

Gladys: Edith Barclay, you know, she used to live at number 6.

Mabel: Edith Barclay! Ooh, I haven't heard from her for **1) donkey's years**! Have she and her son **2) buried the hatchet** yet?

Gladys: Well, that's what she wrote to tell me! Oh, do you remember when Samuel was little? He was **3) the apple of** his mother's **eye** ... and then they fell out when he started seeing that girl ... What was her name?

Mabel: Ooh, Sheila Briggs. Her parents were lovely folk, but she was **4) the black sheep of the family**.

Gladys: I can't see what he saw in her. I remember he chased after her for ages — she really **5) played hard to get**!

Mabel: Yes. And then when they finally started seeing each other he was **6) like putty in her hands** — he even stopped talking to his mother because that girl told him to.

Gladys: Terrible. Anyway, back to the letter ... the Briggs girl must've finally **7) driven him round the bend** — because he broke up with her.

Mabel: Oh good!

Gladys: Yes, and guess what? Edith introduced him to a young lady - Edith said she's a lovely girl. Anyway, apparently they **8) tied the knot** last month and now, what with Sam's good job and all, they're living **9) in clover**!

Mabel: Oh, how lovely. Mind you, I always thought they'd sort it out in the end — after all, **10) blood is thicker than water**.

Gladys: Quite right!

6 Match the items with the idioms from Ex. 5.

a	to pretend one is not interested in sb	g	a long time
b	to annoy sb a lot	h	sb one is most fond of
c	easily controlled or manipulated	i	a person strongly disapproved of by members of his/her family
d	in comfort/wealth	j	blood ties or family relationships are the strongest
e	to get married		
f	to forget old quarrels		

7 Rewrite the following sentences using the words in bold. Do not change these words in any way.

1 Robert and Helen have decided to get married at Christmas.
tie ....
2 It has been ages since I last went to the theatre.
donkey's ....
3 Although David is acting like he's not interested, it's obvious that he likes Mary.
playing ....
4 After years of arguing, the sisters agreed to forget their differences.
hatchet ....
5 Her constant complaining really annoys me.
bend ....

8 Choose the word which best completes each sentence.

1 Anne always does whatever Frank tells her to do. She's like .... in his hands.
A glue   B putty   C butter   D clay

2 Fred was in .... after he won the lottery.
A clover   B grass   C wheat   D barley

3 Perhaps because he was so different, he became the black .... of the family.
A cow   B cat   C sheep   D donkey

4 Laura thinks her son can do no wrong — he's the apple of her ....
A eye   B ear   C heart   D mind

5 Why not ask your family for a loan — after all, blood is .... than water.
A denser   B heavier   C thinner   D thicker

9 Rewrite the following sentences using the words in bold. Do not change these words in any way.

1 No, Mary is not my girlfriend. She is someone I used to go out with.
flame ....

2 Isn't it nice to see a young couple so much in love?
head ....

3 After they won the lottery, they lived comfortably for the rest of their lives.
clover ....

4 My wife and I disagree about keeping a dog.
eye ....

5 He tricked her into marrying him, but then I suppose it's alright because he loves her.
war ....

6 After ten years of living together, they finally got married.
knot ....

7 I think Ann really likes Charles but she is pretending not to be interested.
hard ....

8 Sally has made Geoff go on a diet. Geoff does anything she wants.
putty ....

9 You haven't spoken to your sister for a month. It's time you forgot your disagreement.
hatchet ....

10 Tom really loves Claire. She's the most important person in his life.
apple ....

10 Fill in the gaps with phrases from the list:

bee's knees	black sheep of the family
donkey's years	man of my dreams
stolen his heart	broke my heart
thicker than water	wears his heart on his sleeve
change of heart	round the bend

1 He ....; anyone can see how much he loves her.

2 Bill's really annoying to share a flat with. He's driving me ....

3 She seems to have ....; I hope she doesn't break it.

4 I have been working here for ....

5 Ever since Debbie got the leading role in the play, she thinks she's the ....

6 I always support my brother in arguments. After all, blood is ....

7 Uncle Mark dropped out of school and has never had a steady job. He's the ....

8 The headmaster has had a .... and he isn't going to expel you after all.

9 He's tall, dark, handsome, a millionaire and he wants to marry me. He's the ....

10 Yvonne .... when she left me for Adrian.

11 Answer the questions below:

1 Would you expect to find **the black sheep of the family** living **in clover**? Why/Why not?

2 If you were **the apple of somebody's eye**, would they be **like putty in your hands**? Why/Why not?

3 Would it be wise for two people who don't **see eye to eye** to **tie the knot**? Why/Why not?

4 If you **wear your heart on your sleeve**, are you likely to **have your heart broken**? Why/Why not?

12 This couple has just heard that their daughter is planning on getting married. Using some of the idioms below, discuss possible reasons why they look angry.

- head over heels in love
- the man of her dreams
- all is fair in love and war
- to tie the knot
- the black sheep of the family
- the bee's knees
- to steal sb's heart
- to see eye to eye
- to drive sb round the bend
- blood is thicker than water
- the apple of sb's eye

1 Read the dialogue and try to explain the idioms in bold. Then, look at the picture and say which idiom it represents.

Charles: So James, how's the business doing?

James: Not so good, old boy! I've been having problems with old Rumpton. I'm afraid I'm going to have to **1) give him the boot**.

Charles: Rumpton! But he's been running the factory for years!

James: Yes Charles, I know, but he's getting on a bit you know. He's sixty-two and, quite frankly, I don't think he knows what he's doing anymore. He seems to have turned into **2) a lame duck** in recent years — no control over the workforce and, well, between you and me, the company's **3) feeling the pinch**. You know our profits are down twenty per cent since last year.

Charles: Goodness me! You're not **4) in the red** are you?

James: Certainly not! We haven't **5) hit rock bottom** just yet! No, we don't owe anyone anything. We're still **6) in the black** — for now, at least.

Charles: Well, it sounds like you're **7) playing with fire** if you keep him for much longer! You definitely need to get somebody else to **8) step into his shoes**.

James: Yes, but who? I need somebody who's going to run the place with **9) a firm hand** — not take any nonsense, you know?

Charles: Yes, quite. Do be careful though, old chap. A hasty decision won't **10) pay dividends**, believe me!

2 Match the items with the idioms from Ex. 1.

a	in debt	f	a person/company that is weak/a failure
b	in credit/making profit	g	to bring advantages at a later date
c	to replace sb	h	control and discipline
d	to reach the lowest point	i	to take dangerous risks
e	to suffer because of lack of money	j	to fire sb from their job

3 Fill in the gaps with phrases from the list:

a lame duck, in the red, in the black, a firm hand, playing with fire

1 You should stop spending so much money or you'll be .... before you know it!

2 There are very few problems at this school as the headmaster governs the students with ....
....

3 Tom's new business turned out to be .... and he lost a lot of money.

4 Gayle felt relieved when she put her wages into the bank as she was finally .... again.

5 You are .... if you quit your job before finding another one.

4 Fill in the missing verbs to complete the idioms. Then, choose any three and make sentences.

1 to .... rock bottom
2 to .... the pinch
3 to .... dividends
4 to .... sb the boot
5 to .... into sb's shoes

5 Read the extract from a story and try to explain the idioms in bold.

"What? Another loan? No way, Kim. I've already given you **1) a small fortune!**" Kim shuddered as she knew her father **2) meant business** this time; she could hear it in his voice.

"But, Dad... Please! Just until I **3) get** the company **off the ground**. Once I get some orders I'll be fine... Honest!" She was desperate. Unless her father helped her out, her new clothing company would never get the chance to **4) bear fruit**. "I'm **5) living on a shoestring** already; all I get is my income support!" She could hear her father trying to interrupt, but she went on, "Listen, I've been **6) burning the midnight oil** this month and I'm exhausted, but I've figured out that just another thousand should do it. You'll see!"

"I said no, Kim," her father stated sternly. "You seem to think that I **7) am rolling in it**, but I'm not — I work hard to earn the little that I do, and to be honest, I'm not sure if I'll be able to **8) keep my head above water** if I keep lending you money." Kim fought back a sob. She couldn't believe that he would let her down.

"I'm begging you, Dad. It won't be **9) money down the drain**. Just give me a chance to show you! You'll get it all back with interest!" Kim waited nervously for her father's reply. Eventually, he answered.

"Alright love. But this is the last time. I hope that you realise that your mother and I are really going to have to **10) tighten our belts** though."

6 Match the items with the idioms from Ex. 5.

a	to manage with very little money	e	a lot of money
b	to live on a smaller budget	f	money wasted
c	to be serious about what one says/intends	g	to survive despite financial problems
d	to work very late at night to achieve sth	h	to produce good results
		i	to be rich
		j	to start a business/ company/project, etc

7 Rewrite the following sentences using the words in bold. Do not change these words in any way.

1 During the economic crisis, even the royal family had to spend less money than usual.
belts ....

2 Money is so scarce at the moment that I have had to take a second job just to survive.
water ....

3 I knew that Ray had been working late as he looked exhausted.
oil ....

4 I knew that Mrs Watkin was serious when I got a letter from her lawyer.
business ....

5 It costs a lot of money to start a business.
ground ....

8 Fill in the phrases from the list.

money down the drain, live on a shoestring, rolling in it, bear fruit, a small fortune

Peter: Susan, I have the most wonderful news!

Susan: What is it? What's happened?

Peter: All the hard work we put into our formula is about to 1)........................... .
Someone wants to market it. We'll be rich. We won't have to 2) .... any more.

Susan: That's wonderful, darling. I knew that it wasn't 3) .... when we put all our savings into improving the formula. It'll earn us 4).. .

Peter: You are right, dear. Let's go out and celebrate. After all, soon we'll be 5) ....

9   **Fill in the gaps with phrases from the list:**

meant business, given the boot, hit rock bottom, rolling in it, living on a shoestring, a lame duck, pay dividends, tighten her belt, step into his shoes, head above water

1   With what little money I have from my savings, I can barely keep my ....

2   The rent on Vicky's new flat is very high, so she'll have to .... from now on.

3   The long hours and hard work we put into the new company are finally beginning to ....

4   Ross is such an irresponsible employee; I wouldn't be surprised if he is .... soon.

5   Arthur's off sick for a few months. So, Jenny, you'll have to ....

6   Nora's .... as a secretary. She can't do the job and is an expense to the company.

7   The company .... after all the investors suddenly pulled out.

8   We've been .... all winter so that we can afford to get married in August.

9   The public realised that the new government .... as soon as it raised the nation's taxes.

10 You could ask your boss to buy you a new company car; after all he's ....

10   **Rewrite the following sentences using the words in bold. Do not change these words in any way.**

1   It's a good idea to take out a small loan to help start your business.
    ground   ....

2   For the first time in years, IHD Industries is making a profit.
    black   ....

3   Young offenders need strict guidance to help them reform.
    firm   ....

4   You'll have to work late tonight in order to finish the project.
    oil   ....

5   People have been suffering financially since the government raised taxes.
    pinch   ....

6   The company's investment in computer design is now producing good results.
    fruit   ....

7   Money spent on the National Lottery is just money wasted.
    drain   ....

8   If you're in debt, you should get another job.
    red   ....

9   My family lost a huge amount of money in the stock market crash of 1929.
    fortune   ....

10 You're taking a big risk if you borrow money to buy stocks and shares.
    fire   ....

11   **Say whether the idioms in the sentences below are used correctly or incorrectly. Then replace the incorrect idioms with a suitable alternative.**

1   She **was given the boot** last week and now she has to find another job.

2   I'm afraid you're **in the black** again, Mr Jones — you owe the bank £500.

3   Helen was **a lame duck** when she sold her property at a great profit.

4   Many students **live on a shoestring** while they are at university.

5   In my opinion, buying a second-hand car is just **money down the drain**.

6   Our company finally started to **hit rock bottom** after its fourth year in business and we paid off our loan.

7   After Anna's father retired, she **stepped into his shoes** and became the director of the family business.

8   I knew my rival **tightened his belt** when I received a call from his lawyer.

9   You've been **playing with fire** again, haven't you? You haven't stopped yawning all morning.

10 We really **felt the pinch** after spending so much money on our new house.

Unit 4

1 Read the review and try to explain the idioms in bold. Then, look at the picture and say which idiom it represents.

In this week's guide to eating out in the city, John Boyd reviews the hottest new restaurant in town:

The Stadium

Now, here's **1) food for thought** — a restaurant-cum-sports museum. "It'll never work," I thought to myself as I made my way to ex-rugby international Ray Plum's new restaurant to join a group of friends for a birthday dinner. However, as soon as I stepped through the door into the delicious food smells, which certainly **2) whetted my appetite,** and the fantastic décor, which consisted entirely of sport's memorabilia from floor to ceiling, I was **3) at a loss for words**!

We were ushered to our table by a friendly waiter who then left us to look at the menu. The dish descriptions **4) made our mouths water** and soon we were enjoying our meal. The chef clearly hadn't **5) cut** any **corners**, as the ingredients were of the highest quality.

Later on in the evening, when the birthday celebrations were **6) in full swing**, I managed to **7) pull a few strings** to see the kitchen as I knew the manager's son. I have to say that other chefs **8) cannot hold a candle to** the way in which *The Stadium's* chef runs his kitchen.

Shortly before we left, our birthday girl insisted on **9) picking up the tab.** I was pleasantly surprised, on taking a peek at the total, to calculate that it had only come to £12 per person.

I for one shall certainly be paying another visit to *The Stadium* just to **10) feast my eyes on** the décor, the fantastic old sporting photos and memorabilia. It is certainly a place well worth visiting.

2 Match the items with the idioms from Ex. 1.

a	to make sb keen to experience/taste more of sth	**f**	unable to think of anything to say
b	to use a cheaper/easier method	**g**	to cause sb to desire sth, especially food
c	at a very lively stage/point	**h**	cannot be compared favourably with sb/sth
d	to look with pleasure at sth/sb	**i**	to use influence to achieve sth
e	to pay for sth	**j**	sth to think about

3 Fill in the gaps with phrases from the list:

at a loss for words, cut corners, picking up the tab, hold a candle to, whet my appetite

1 Paul .... when building his new house and now he is having trouble with it.
2 The new managing director can't .... his predecessor.
3 Mary was .... when her boss asked her if she'd like to be promoted.
4 I've only read the back of the book, but it was enough to ....
5 Vanessa's parents are .... for her trip to Europe next summer.

4 Fill in the gaps with phrases from the list:

food for thought, feast your eyes on, make your mouth water, pull a few strings, in full swing

Helen: So how was Angela's wedding?
Fiona: Brilliant. Her dress was something to **1)** ....!
Helen: And the reception?
Fiona: It was quite impressive. Fortunately, Tony's dad knows the manager of *The Grand*, so he was able to **2)** .... and arrange to hold the reception there for half the normal price. You know, the menu alone was enough to **3)** ....! Unfortunately, I had to leave while the party was still **4)** .... as I had to get up early for work the next morning — but it's certainly given me **5)** .... for my own wedding!

5 Read the dialogue and try to explain the idioms in bold.

Celia: Hi Rachel.
Rachel: Celia! How was your blind date last night?
Celia: Awful! Roger definitely **1) wasn't my cup of tea**! I don't know why Karen thought I'd like him. Personally I think she was **2) scraping the bottom of the barrel** — he was incredibly rude, quite horrid, actually!
Rachel: Oh dear. What happened?
Celia: Well, we'd arranged to meet at the *King's Head* for a drink first, you know, to **3) break the ice**. I should have realised I was **4) in the soup** when I heard him speaking to the barmaid — he was so impolite I blushed! And the way he kept shovelling peanuts into his mouth and talking at the same time **5) turned my stomach**.
Rachel: Urgh! How awful!
Celia: Oh, that wasn't all! I'd made a real effort with my hair and make-up and I'd even bought a new dress. He didn't say anything about how nice I looked — talk about **6) casting pearls before swine**! And then, just before we left, he knocked my glass of red wine all over me, and do you know what he said? **7) "It's no use crying over spilt milk."** I should have left there and then! He criticised my car all the way to the restaurant too, said it was uncomfortable and didn't go fast enough, but when I asked him what he drove, he said he didn't!
Rachel: Sounds like **8) sour grapes** to me.
Celia: Quite. Anyway at the restaurant, he started complaining that the meat was **9) as dry as a bone** — it was delicious — and that the service wasn't **10) up to scratch** — it was faultless.
Rachel: So what did you do?
Celia: Well I left, didn't I?

6 Match the items with the idioms from Ex. 5.

a	not to be to one's taste	f	there is no point in regretting sth that has happened
b	to offer sth good to sb who cannot appreciate the value of it	g	to cause sb to feel sick/disgusted
c	negative attitude/bitterness because of jealousy	h	of the desired standard
d	to be left with/use the worst person/object	i	to make sb relax/to get conversation started
e	in trouble	j	very dry

7 Rewrite the following sentences using the words in bold. Do not change these words in any way.

1 I've been going to the same restaurant for years, but lately it hasn't been up to the standard it should be.
scratch ....
2 Camping in the wilderness doesn't appeal to Greg.
cup ....
3 You forgot to water my plants! Look, the soil is very dry.
bone ....
4 Ross was nervous when he went for his job interview, but the director put him at ease by making a joke.
ice ....
5 Roxanne was in trouble when she crashed her father's car.
soup ....

8 Choose the word which best completes each sentence.

1 The thought of eating raw fish turns my ....
A head   B stomach   C legs   D belly
2 Jessica was scraping the bottom of the .... for an excuse saying she had a hairdresser's appointment.
A glass   B pitcher   C jug   D barrel
3 Daisy says she didn't want to be chosen, but it's just sour ....; she did really.
A grapes   B lemons   C raisins   D milk
4 Harold realised too late that he had sold the van too cheaply; but there was no point in .... over spilt milk.
A sobbing   B weeping   C screaming   D crying

14

5 Steven tried to teach his son to appreciate opera, but he was just .... pearls before swine.
 A hurling   **B** casting   **C** throwing   **D** tossing

9 Fill in the missing verbs to complete the idioms. Then, choose any five and make sentences.

1 to .... the ice
2 to .... one's appetite
3 to .... one's eyes on
4 to .... the tab
5 to .... pearls before swine
6 to .... sb's stomach
7 to .... sb's mouth water
8 to .... the bottom of the barrel
9 to .... a few strings
10 to .... corners

10 Complete the sentences using a suitable idiom. Keep the meaning the same as in the given sentence.

1 Unfortunately, the electricity went off at the best part of the concert.
 Unfortunately, the electricity went off when the concert was... .
2 Tim didn't know what to say when he heard he had won the prize.
 Tim was .... when he heard he had won the prize.
3 If you're having problems with your landlord, you can come and stay with me.
 If you're .... with your landlord, you can come and stay with me.
4 Charles Johnson's new film will certainly give you something to think about.
 Charles Johnson's new film will certainly be
 ....
5 I don't like abstract art; I think it's ugly.
 Abstract art is ....; I think it's ugly.
6 The soil here gets little water so no plants can grow.
 The soil here is ....
 so no plants can grow.
7 My teacher told me that my essay wasn't good enough.
 My teacher told me that my essay wasn't ....
 ....
8 Jane said that she hated my new dress, but I'm sure she would have loved to have one just like it.

Jane said that she hated my new dress, but I'm sure it was just ....
9 This new government is nowhere near as good as the previous one.
 This new government can't ....
 the previous one.
10 When his bike was stolen, Mike said it wasn't worth grieving over.
 When his bike was stolen, Mike said it was ....
 ....

11 a) Look at the pictures below and say which idioms are represented.

b) Now, use the idioms to complete the following sentences.

1 James knew he would be .... when he realised he was an hour late for the rendezvous.
2 Kim said Clara's new earrings made her look silly, but it was just .... because Clara would have loved to have a pair herself.
3 When we went to summer camp, there was a party on the first night to help ....
4 That cake smells delicious. It's really ....
 ....
5 My family don't appreciate art so it was like ....
 .... when I took them to the Monet exhibition.
6 If you .... when building a house, it will not be safe to live in.

1 Read the advertisement and try to explain the idioms in bold. Then, look at the picture and say which idiom it represents.

DOCTOR HERBERT´S CURE-ALL LIFE TONIC

Unlike some "remedies", whose creators' claims have to **1) be taken with a pinch of salt**, DR HERBERT´S LIFE TONIC IS NO GIMMICK!

Whether you´re **2) at death´s door** or simply feeling a bit **3) off colour**, Dr Herbert´s Life Tonic will have you feeling **4) full of beans** again in no time. But don´t just take our word for it. Mr Jethro Franklin of Dodgeville, Texas had been suffering from heart problems and severe back pains for over ten years, before he turned to Dr Herbert for help.

"I had been **5) going downhill** for a long, long time before I came to Dr Herbert. I had lost so much weight that I was **6) nothing but skin and bone**, and on most days I couldn't even get out of bed in the mornings! However, Dr Herbert´s Life Tonic changed all that. I was just **7) a shadow of my former self** when I started taking his Life Tonic, but I was **8) up and about** again in just two weeks. That was just six months ago and now I feel **9) as strong as an ox** - in fact, after giving me just three months to live last year, my doctor now says that I should live to a **10) ripe old age!**"

DON´T DELAY! FOR THE CURE-ALL REMEDY, GET DR HERBERT´S LIFE TONIC TODAY!

2 Match the items with the idioms from Ex. 1.

a unwell	**f** active after an illness
b very thin	**g** very lively and energetic
c to get worse in health/ quality/status, etc	**h** very strong and fit
d about to die	**i** weaker or less capable than one used to be
e to be doubted/considered untrue	**j** very old age

3 Fill in the gaps with phrases from the list:

go downhill, pinch of salt, up and about, ripe old age, off colour

1 As soon as your leg is out of the cast, you'll be ....
.... in no time.
2 John has a reputation for being a liar, so whenever he tells me anything, I take it with a ....
3 Peter didn't go to school today because he was feeling a bit ....
4 The recession will affect industry badly and many companies will ....
5 My grandfather lived to a .... He was 104 years old when he passed away.

4 Fill in the gaps with phrases from the list:

as strong as an ox, full of beans, but skin and bone, at death's door, a shadow of his former self

Mary: Hello Mr Herriot. I was wondering if you could have a look at Fido, my dog. He's usually so **1)** .... but he's been refusing his food for a week now and, well, look at him, he's nothing **2)** ....

Vet: Let me see now. Oh dear, he's just **3)** ...., isn't he? Let's have a look ... hmm, yes, I think I know what it is. Don't worry — I don't think he's **4)** .... just yet!

Mary: So what is it Mr Herriot?

Vet: Just a stomach bug, dear. Give him one of these tablets three times a day and he should be **5)** .... in a week or so.

5 Read the dialogue and try to explain the idioms in bold.

Frank: Hey Jack! Here, you´ll never guess what I heard yesterday.

Jack: What?

Frank: Old Trevor´s **1) kicked the bucket.**

Jack: No! But I saw him out with the dog just last week and he was **2) alive and kicking** then!

Frank: Well, you know, appearances can be deceptive. Apparently it had been **3) touch and go** as to whether his heart would keep going since last year when he had all those problems.

Jack: Oh blast! I had no idea. Poor Trevor. How´s your brother?

Frank: Ah yes, Donald. Well, the doctors reckon **4) the writing is on the wall** for him too, but he seems to be **5) holding his own**. I saw him just last night at Reg´s and he can still beat me at poker - the old rascal was **6) grinning from ear to ear** when I left! No, I´m pretty certain **7) there´s life in the old dog yet**. But what about Betty? Are her eyes still bad?

Jack: Yes, they´ve got worse, she´s **8) as blind as a bat** now. Mind you, the kids have been great, they seem to think that both me and their mum **9) have got one foot in the grave**, so they´ve been helping out a lot with the shopping and cleaning and stuff. I´ll tell you what though ...

Frank: What?

Jack: I just hope they don´t **10) run out of steam** before I do!

6 Match the items with the idioms from Ex. 5.

a	to be near death	**f**	a sign/warning of danger/unhappiness/failure, etc
b	blind or unable to see well	**g**	to die
c	still alive and active	**h**	to manage despite difficulties/obstacles
d	one is still physically/mentally energetic despite old age	**i**	to smile broadly
e	uncertain	**j**	to lose the energy that one had previously

7 Rewrite the following sentences replacing the words in bold with phrases from the list.

kick the bucket, am as blind as a bat, grinned from ear to ear, there's life in the old dog yet, run out of steam

1 Without my glasses I **can't see anything**.

....
....

2 If I don't have a cup of coffee with my lunch, I **become weak and faint** by three o'clock.

....
....

3 Everyone thinks that Mr Jones is about to **die**, but **he's still alright in spite of his age**.

....
....

4 When Cathy heard that she had been promoted, she **had a huge smile on her face**.

....
....

8 Fill in the gaps with phrases from the list:

one foot in the grave, touch and go, alive and kicking, writing was on the wall, held his own

John: I was amazed to see Gerald back at work.

David: Yes, me too. When he was in hospital it was **1)** .... for a while, according to the doctors.

John: That's right. Two weeks ago it looked like the **2)** ....; he had **3)** ....

David: Apparently it was just a virus. All he needed was a long rest.

John: Well, he **4)** ...., didn't he?

David: I'll say! He's certainly **5)** .... now!

9   Fill in the gaps with phrases from the list:

ripe old age, held our own, there's life in the old dog yet, touch and go, up and about, at death's door, took it with a pinch of salt, as strong as an ox, writing is on the wall, a shadow of his former self

1   The patient might not survive; it's .... for now, I'm afraid.
2   The .... for the factory. It will probably close next year.
3   We lost the debate although we .... in all the arguments.
4   After the take-over we were told to expect a pay rise but we ....
5   We were surprised to see James .... only two weeks after his operation.
6   Bill isn't weak at all; in fact, he's ....
7   Mr Marshall has recovered unexpectedly, so it seems ....
8   Matthew never really got over his road accident. He's been .... ever since.
9   She survived until the .... of 92.
10 When the old man realised he was ...., he asked to see a priest.

10   Rewrite the following sentences using the words in bold. Do not change these words in any way.

1   You don't look very well, I think you should go home.
    colour   ....
2   Jason has a big smile in all the wedding photographs.
    ear   ....
3   I suddenly became very tired while shopping and had to sit down and have a coffee.
    steam   ....
4   John's work deteriorated rapidly after he fell ill.
    downhill ....
5   You know, Geoff can't see a thing without his glasses.
    bat   ....
6   Let's face it, Kate Moss is very thin!
    bone   ....
7   We haven't heard from Marion for a while, but Tim tells me she's fit and healthy.
    alive   ....
8   We all thought Rachel had died until she leapt up and started laughing at us.
    bucket   ....

9   I went for a swim early this morning and I've felt energetic all day.
    beans   ....
10 We thought Sir John was almost ready to die but he was just pretending to be ill.
    foot   ....

11   Answer the questions below:

1   Can somebody be **alive and kicking** after they **have kicked the bucket**? Why/Why not?
2   Can you be **full of beans** and **off colour** at the same time? Why/Why not?
3   When somebody tells you something serious while they are **grinning from ear to ear** should you **take it with a pinch of salt**? Why/Why not?
4   Could **there be life in the old dog yet** even if he were **as blind as a bat**? Why/Why not?
5   If a doctor told you that someone's condition was **touch and go** after an operation, would you be surprised to see the person **up and about** the next day? Why/Why not?
6   Do you think that the fax machine will continue to **hold its own** in this era of electronic mail? Why/Why not?

12   Use the idioms in the list to talk about the man in the picture below.

full of beans, as strong as an ox, at death's door, a shadow of his former self, ripe old age, to run out of steam

Unit 6

1 Read the newspaper review of a film and try to explain the idioms in bold.

Viewer's Choice

TUMBLE (James Reed 1972) BBC 2 10:45 pm

James Reed's classic production, starring Chuck Williams, Jay Johnson and Glenda Moore, tells the tale of a man who rises to **1) the top of the ladder**, before ending up as a **2) down-and-out** begging for money and **3) living rough** on the streets of New York.

At the beginning of the story, we meet Charlie Renton (Chuck Williams) who is **4) as poor as a church mouse** and lives in a tiny basement flat in Brooklyn. By luck, he manages to get a job with a big exporting company, and so begins his rapid rise **5) from rags to riches**.

Quickly, the **6) up-and-coming** young business-man becomes the company director's **7) right hand man** and miraculously helps the firm to double its profits in just one year. Then, following the retirement of his superior (Jay Johnson), Charlie finds himself **8) calling the shots** in the company.

For a while, everything seems fine: Charlie marries Charlene (Glenda Moore), moves into a fantastic house and joins **9) the jet set** with their extravagant parties, exclusive country clubs and flashy sports cars. Unfortunately, it is at this point that his slide down **10) the slippery slope** towards self-destruction begins.

Tumble is a magnificently directed study of human behaviour with a highly talented cast. Be prepared for some tear-jerking scenes, but don't miss it.

2 Match the items with the idioms from Ex. 1.

a	the highest position in one's profession	**f**	group of rich and fashionable people who are interested in enjoyment
b	from being very poor to being very rich		
c	sth that is difficult to stop once it has begun and which usually ends badly	**g**	likely to become successful
		h	person with no job or home
d	close and trusted assistant	**i**	to live under unpleasant conditions
e	to make the important decisions	**j**	extremely poor

3 Fill in the gaps with phrases from the list:

poor as a church mouse, jet set, calling the shots, right hand man, up-and-coming

1 I couldn't manage at work without Baxter — he's my
....
2 Now that the director has retired, Fred Martin will be taking over and ....
3 Sven can't even afford to buy a bus ticket — he's as
....
4 No wonder Carlos is regarded as the best ....
.... artist — his paintings are fantastic!
5 Now that his business is successful, Errol has joined the ....; he's bought houses in France and Tahiti.

4 Fill in the gaps with phrases from the list:

the slippery slope, from rags to riches, down-and-out, lives rough, the top of the ladder

John came from a poor family in South London, but thanks to his shrewd business sense he went **1)** .... and became a very successful stockbroker. Unfortunately, while he was at **2)** .... he started drinking heavily and thus began his descent down **3)** .... towards homelessness and poverty.

Today John **4)** .... in the door-ways and alley-ways of central London. Little did he know, at the peak of his career, that he would end up a **5)** ...., even poorer than he had been before.

5 Read the dialogue and try to explain the idioms in bold.

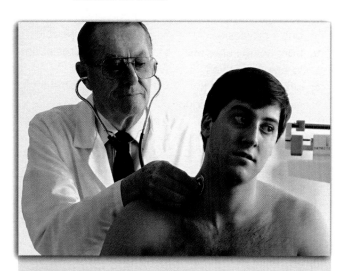

Bryson: So Doctor, is it serious?
Doctor: Yes, Mr Bryson, I'm afraid it is. Have you been under a lot of pressure recently?
Bryson: As the head of a multinational company? I'll say! You see, we **1) have got several irons in the fire** at the moment — we're in the process of closing six major deals — so everyone's working **2) at full stretch**, including me, of course.
Doctor: Hm, yes. I saw you talking about buying out Swift Airlines on the news last night. Are you sure it would be wise to take over such an ailing company? It sounds like a bit of **3) a dead end** to me. Anyway, back to your chest pains. First of all, you ought to **4) adopt a lower profile** — all this publicity must be rather stressful. You really should **5) take a back seat** in the company.
Bryson: What? Let somebody else step into my shoes?
Doctor: Yes. Actually, the best thing you could do would be to leave **6) the rat race** altogether.
Bryson: Ah, Dr Morley, life isn't that easy when you're one of **7) the big guns**; I've got far too much responsibility. Mind you, it would be lovely to **8) have time on my hands** — I'd be able to go fishing and see the children more often. Yes, it would be nice to **9) do my own thing** for a while.
Doctor: So why don't you?
Bryson: Let me put it like this: Margaret's been pestering me to buy an apartment in Paris like the Bransons', and a yacht like the Guinness's, so I suppose I'll have to keep working just so she can **10) keep up with the Joneses!**
Doctor: Yes, well. Now, seriously Mr Bryson, unless you start taking it easy soon, you won't be much use to anyone.

6 Match the items with the idioms from Ex. 5.

a sth which leads no-where and has no future	**f** the struggle for success, especially in a large city
b using all one's energy to do sth	**g** to be in competition with other people for a higher social standard
c to avoid public attention	**h** to have spare time
d important and powerful people	**i** to do whatever one wants
e to have several options/ projects at the same time	**j** to take a position of less importance /influence

7 Rewrite the following sentences using the words in bold. Do not change these words in any way.

1 The researchers had to work very hard for six months in order to complete the project.
stretch ....

2 The politician seems to be avoiding the cameras since his unfortunate public display.
low ....

3 Selling encyclopedias over the telephone is a job with no future — you should look for another career.
dead ....

4 Now that Ellen's retired, she has a lot of spare time.
hands ....

5 Greta can't really afford a skiing holiday — she's only going because her friends are.
Joneses ....

8 Choose the word which best completes each sentence.

1 John takes a .... seat in his marriage. His wife makes all the decisions in the family.
A tail **B** rear **C** front **D** back

2 Catherine Rhodes is considered to be one of the big .... in the fashion industry.
A rifles **B** guns **C** pistols **D** weapons

3 The couple decided to leave the .... race and move to a small farm in the country instead.
A human **B** rodent **C** rat **D** mouse

4 When Tim moved out of his parents' house he was able to .... his own thing.
A do **B** be **C** have **D** get

5 Martha didn't get the job at the florist's, but she's got several .... in the fire.

A logs B irons C coals D embers

9 Say whether the idioms in the sentences below are used correctly or incorrectly. Then replace the incorrect idioms with a suitable alternative.

1 Because the company's vice president was such a skilled negotiator, the president preferred to **do his own thing** in important business transactions.
2 As the international peace talks were **calling the shots** the leaders of several countries decided to walk out.
3 Brad had no money when he arrived in London, so he was forced to **live rough.**
4 I decided to get out of **the jet set** when my job started to affect my marriage.
5 Although Barbara is only thirty, she is considered to be the **up-and-coming** new lawyer in the firm.
6 After working **at the top of the ladder** for three months, the fashion house produced its fantastic autumn collection.
7 The director wouldn't know what to do if it weren't for his **right hand man.**
8 Robert's life was a typical **rags-to-riches** story — as a child he was very poor but by the time he died, he was a millionaire.
9 Now I have **many irons in the fire,** I think I'll go on a relaxing long holiday.
10 Even though they didn't need an expensive car, the Martins bought one just to **keep up with the Joneses.**

10 Fill in the missing verbs to complete the idioms. Then, choose any four and make sentences.

1 to .... a back seat
2 to .... the shots
3 to .... a low profile
4 to .... many/several irons in the fire
5 to .... rough
6 to .... one's own thing

11 a. Look at the pictures below and say which idioms are represented.

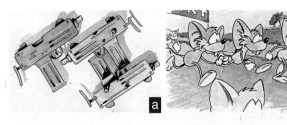

b. Look at the newspaper headlines below and replace the words in bold with idioms from section a. above.

Business Tycoon Claims To Have **Many Projects in Progress**

1 ....

Middle East Delegates **To Give The Orders** Over Arms Sales

2 ....

Industrial **Leaders** To Attend Environmental Talks in Geneva

3 ....

Pop Star to Retire After **Winning "Best Singer" Award**

4 ....

Leading Businessman Announces Tired of **Fierce Competition** In Modern Life

5 ....

1 Read the article and try to explain the idioms in bold.

Though environmentally-friendly vehicle inventors have had little success in their attempts to **1) break the mould** of conventional car design up until now, it seems likely that things are about to change and that pollution-free cars may soon become **2) all the rage**. In fact, it is now quite possible that the age of hydropower is **3) just around the corner**, thanks to the creators of the Nexus Aqua Car who have **4) broken new ground** in the production of 'clean' vehicles.

It appears that the petrol-guzzlers that we drive today may soon become **5) old hat** as the Aqua Car is **6) the last word** in non-toxic technology. The concept originated in 1994 when Nexus Motors hired a team of scientists to work on the creation of a vehicle that would be completely harmless to the environment. Today, they have succeeded in producing an aesthetically pleasing, **7) state-of-the-art** machine that will satisfy the needs of speed fiends and conservationists alike. Indeed, not only is this vehicle powerful (the Aqua Car has a top speed of 190 mph), attractive and environmentally friendly, but it also has a range of new accessories, including automatic steering and an 'in-car route guide', which are **8) streets ahead** of the competition.

Nexus expects to have the Aqua Car in showrooms by next September, which can only mean there is trouble **9) on the horizon** for both the petrol industry and conventional car manufacturers. The latter will undoubtedly be forced to start redesigning their vehicles **10) from scratch**.

2 Match the items with the idioms from Ex. 1.

a	very close in time/ distance	f	old-fashioned
b	to develop sth/ to make innovations	g	using the most modern techniques
c	to completely change the way sth is done	h	more advanced
d	from the beginning and without any help	i	expected/likely to happen soon
e	the best/most recent version of sth	j	very popular/ fashionable

3 Fill in the gaps with phrases from the list:

streets ahead, last word, state-of-the-art, from scratch, broke the mould

1 The bank has a .... security system.
2 Margaret Thatcher .... of British politics by becoming the country's first female prime minister.
3 This computer is .... of all the others on the market.
4 When their house burnt down, the Nishes built a new one ....
5 Tony's new car is the .... in comfort.

4 Fill in the gaps with phrases from the list:

around the corner, old hat, on the horizon, broken new ground, all the rage

Sam: Do you like my new cassette recorder?
Jenny: Oh Sam! Cassette recorders are **1)**..............
.... now. Didn't you know that CDs are **2)** .... today? They've really **3)** .... in music technology.
Sam: Really? But what about all my cassettes?
Jenny: Sam! You have to realise that the decline of the cassette recorder is **4)** .... and what with more sophisticated CD models just **5)** .... you'd best forget your cassettes!

5 Read the dialogue and try to explain the idioms in bold.

Ruth: Darling, I've come to the conclusion that this car is **1) past it**. It's hopeless ... I mean, look; we're on the motorway and you can't even get it up to sixty!

John: Oh, come on, love. It's fine, and this model has certainly **2) stood the test of time**. Look! There's another one — it's not as if nobody drives them any more! You know what? Back **3) in my day**, this was the best car on the road, and quite frankly, in my opinion these new cars of today just aren't as good.

Ruth: But John, you're **4) living in the past**! Today's cars are much better and safer too! Take Volvos for example, they're just as sturdy as this, and the new models have sunroofs, power steering, airbags — you name it! Face it, this car is **5) as old as the hills** and sooner or later you're going to have to buy a **6) brand new** one.

John: Brand new, eh? Do you know how much they cost? Oh, I wish we could **7) turn the clock back** to 1964; you could buy a new car for £500, then.

Ruth: Okay, okay. Just a slightly more **8) up-to-date** one, then. But you've got to **9) move with the times**, and I've heard you can get a good second-hand car for around £3,000.

John: Listen Ruth. There is nothing wrong with this car. You can nag me **10) till the cows come home**, but I'm not going to buy a new car until I'm ready to.

Ruth: John? ... Is that smoke coming out of the engine?

John: What? ... Oh blast!

6 Match the items with the idioms from Ex. 5.

a	too old to work well or safely	**f**	completely new
b	very old	**g**	to go back in time, especially to sth now considered old-fashioned
c	to behave as if what existed in the past still exists	**h**	for a long time
d	to progress with changing customs/ fashions, etc	**i**	modern/new
e	to prove reliable/valuable over a long period	**j**	at a time in the past when sb/sth was young/popular/ successful, etc

7 Choose the word which best completes each sentence.

1 Your television is ancient. Why not sell it and get something more up to .... ?
   A now   **B** present   **C** date   **D** time

2 Shakespeare's plays have stood the .... of time because they are so well-written.
   A test   **B** quiz   **C** exam   **D** road

3 In my ...., children were seen and not heard.
   A times   **B** moment   **C** day   **D** life

4 Although they are still young, most models are considered .... it by the age of 30.
   A beyond   **B** over   **C** after   **D** past

5 If I could turn the .... back, I would do things differently.
   A clock   **B** watch   **C** hours   **D** years

8 Rewrite the following sentences using the words in bold. Do not change these words in any way.

1 My computer is completely new. I only bought it this morning.
   brand ....

2 Jane's father would be quite happy to talk about politics forever.
   cows ....

3 Your washing-machine is very old. Perhaps it's time you bought a new one.
   hills ....

4 Stop behaving as if things hadn't changed since you were a young man, Roy. Don't you realise we're in the 1990s?
   past ....

5 The company needs to progress; that's the reason why they're installing computers.
   times ....

9   Match the sentences below:

1 Gordon's birthday is just around the corner.
2 Bill's fridge is past it.
3 Mobile phones seem to be all the rage now.
4 Terry will have to write another composition from scratch.
5 Fred is living in the past.
6 Uncle Ted said that women never wore trousers back in his day.
7 Craig's computer is streets ahead of mine.
8 With war on the horizon, Will realised he might have to enlist.
9 James wanted to turn the clock back.
10 Martin said he could eat apple pie till the cows come home.

a Everybody has got one.
b But that was a long time ago.
c You'd better buy him a present soon.
d It's the best model in the shops.
e He still thinks it's okay to leave his door unlocked.
f Six months later he was asked to join the army.
g I think he should replace it.
h He wished he had never left his wife.
i He likes it a lot.
j His mother accidentally threw it away.

10   Look at the two pictures below. Using some of the idioms from the list, compare and contrast the two buildings.

brand new, to break new ground, to break the mould, the last word, as old as the hills, old hat, to move with the times, to stand the test of time, state-of-the-art

11   Use the words missing from the sentences below to complete the crossword.

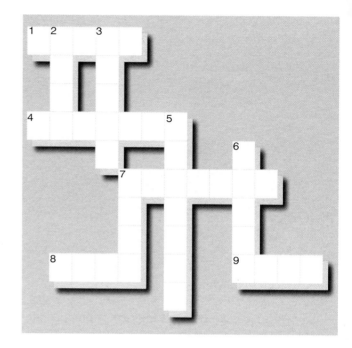

Across

1 We've just had a .... -of-the-art heating system installed in our house.
4 This new fax machine is .... ahead of the older models.
7 Researchers claim that a cure for cancer is on the ....
8 Flared trousers were all the .... during the 1970s.
9 I've exchanged my old cooker for a more up-to- .... model.

Down

2 *Gone With The Wind* has stood the .... of time — it's still a classic.
3 Mike's learning how to use a computer. He feels he ought to move with the ....
5 Jim's uncle built his boat from ....
6 The headmaster broke the .... of traditional teaching by introducing computers into every lesson.
7 You can beg me to lend you the car till the cows come .... I'll still say no!

1 Read the text and try to explain the idioms in bold.

Our expedition up Mont Blanc had been plagued by difficulties from the start, and we had just decided to make a **1) last-ditch** attempt for the summit when we noticed that the weather was deteriorating. After much discussion, we decided that we should **2) cut our losses** and return to base camp. Little did we realise, though, that the worsening weather conditions were just **3) the tip of the iceberg**.

As we were approaching the half-way point, we realised that a large part of the cliff face had **4) vanished into thin air**, taking with it the narrow path we had used on our way up. It was at this point that several less experienced members of the team started to panic and it looked as though the situation might get **5) out of hand**. I knew we would **6) not have a hope in hell** if we all stayed there waiting for a rescue party to come and **7) lend a hand**, so I told our terrified colleagues to **8) sit tight** while three of us attempted to climb down the mountain.

We suffered our next **9) close call** about three quarters of the way down when our rope snapped, leaving us clinging to the rock. We had two choices: we could stay there and freeze to death or we could attempt to descend without ropes — we decided to **10) chance it** and climb down.

Three hours later we reached base camp. From there we were able to inform the mountain rescue service of where the others were and, before nightfall, they too were safe.

2 Match the items with the idioms from Ex. 1.

a	the tiniest sign of a larger problem	**g**	not to change one's position/to stay where one is
b	a close encounter with danger	**h**	final (attempt/effort, etc)
c	to have no chance	**i**	to help
d	to disappear completely	**j**	to give up doing sth so as to limit/prevent further loss/damage
e	to take a risk		
f	out of control		

3 Fill in the missing verbs to complete the idioms. Then, choose any three and make sentences.

1 to .... tight

2 to .... one's losses

3 to .... a hand

4 to .... it

5 not to .... a hope in hell

4 Fill in the gaps with phrases from the list:

last-ditch, close call, vanished into thin air, out of hand, tip of the iceberg

1 The police arrived at the scene of the crime as soon as they could but the robbers had ....

2 The situation at the office has got completely .... since the rumours of a take-over started.

3 Steven had a .... today as he was driving to work — someone went through a red light and almost hit him.

4 In a .... effort to save the old library from being demolished, the residents picketed the Town Hall.

5 The sacking of the part-time staff was just the ....; the company later went bankrupt leaving all the staff out of work.

5 Read the interview and try to explain the idioms in bold.

— Last year, the tiny island of Rosha was devastated by Hurricane Boris, which left 50 people dead and many more injured and homeless. Nine months later, the island's residents were still **1) picking up the pieces** when Hurricane Carloff struck, killing even more people and forcing the survivors **2) back to square one**. With me now, is Rhona Bryce who survived the second hurricane **3) by the skin of her teeth** after her husband dug her out from the rubble of their home **4) with his bare hands**. Mrs Bryce, how are you and your husband coping now?

— Well, we're lucky to have come through these two disasters **5) safe and sound** unlike many who have lost relatives and suffered horrific injuries, but, like nearly everyone else here, we are homeless. Our government is also **6) in a tight corner** as it spent a lot of money trying to rebuild the island after the first hurricane, so, of course, now we are having to rely on charity.

— So what is being done now?

— Well, one organisation has put up temporary housing for some people in the capital, but the rest of us are still living in tents! They've promised emergency funds, but so far, they simply haven't **7) delivered the goods**. It's almost as if the rest of the world has forgotten about us, which is awful when we **8) have our backs against the wall** like this.

— You sound as if you're **9) at the end of your tether**, Mrs Bryce.

— Yes, unfortunately you're right — we all are. We are desperate for aid and unless somebody helps us soon, I really don't know what will happen. We're tired of begging and quite honestly I feel ready to **10) throw in the towel**.

6 Match the items with the idioms from Ex. 5.

a	safe and uninjured	g	to produce the promised /expected results
b	without tools/machinery, etc	h	to give up
c	only just	i	at the point of losing one's patience
d	to restore a situation after confusion/disaster	j	to be in a desperate situation in which one must struggle to survive
e	in a difficult/awkward situation		
f	back to the beginning		

7 Rewrite the following sentences using the words in bold. Do not change these words in any way.

1 Families of the passengers from the burning aeroplane were relieved to hear that their loved ones were all uninjured and free from danger.
   sound ....

2 With a national strike looming, the government found itself in a difficult situation.
   wall ....

3 Since the disaster, we've been trying to get our lives back to normal.
   pieces ....

4 After several attempts to pass his driving test, Roger gave up and bought a bicycle instead.
   towel ....

5 Doug reached the point where he had no more patience after the neighbour's dog woke him up again, so he called the police.
   tether ....

8 Choose the word which best completes each sentence.

1 When the girl was trapped under the car, a man lifted it with his .... hands and saved her.
   A exposed **B** naked   **C** uncovered **D** bare

2 His original manuscript was not accepted so he had to go back to .... one and rewrite it.
   A level   **B** square   **C** plan   **D** number

3 The chess player managed to fight his way out of a .... corner and win the game.
   A tight   **B** narrow   **C** cramped **D** secure

4 During the earthquake, Susan escaped from the building by the .... of her teeth before it collapsed.
   A enamel   **B** coating **C** skin   **D** hair

5 If Jenkins fails to .... the goods one more time, I'll fire him!
   A deliver   **B** transport **C** convey **D** distribute

9 Rewrite the following sentences using the words in bold. Do not change these words in any way.

1 He couldn't find her anywhere! It was as if she had completely disappeared.

vanished ....

2 The wet patch on the ceiling was just the beginning of our problems.

tip ....

3 We decided to stay where we were until the storm ended.

tight ....

4 The expedition might be dangerous, but I'll take a risk and go anyway.

chance ....

5 The police became nervous when the crowd got too difficult to manage.

out ....

6 The weightlifter made one final attempt at the record before giving up.

last ....

7 The pedestrian only just managed to avoid being hit by the oncoming car.

teeth ....

8 It took many years for the government to get things back to normal after the war.

pick ....

9 The burglar realised he was in a difficult situation when he noticed the guard dog.

tight ....

10 Fill in the gaps with phrases from the list:

a close call, deliver the goods, have a hope in hell, throw in the towel, his bare hands, had his back against the wall, safe and sound, at the end of my tether, go back to square one, lend a hand

1 Tom's a terrible poet; he doesn't .... of winning the poetry competition.

2 Our house collapsed as soon as we had finished building it, so we had to ....

3 Jim's very strong; he can tear a telephone directory in half with ....

4 Janet had .... yesterday; she nearly missed her flight to Boston.

5 Our dog returned home .... after going missing for three days.

6 I couldn't lift the box by myself, so I asked Paula to ....

7 The Fountain Hotel's brochure promises exceptional service, but we found it didn't ....

8 The soldier .... and had no choice but to surrender.

9 I'm ....; I've been trying to fix this tap all day and it still doesn't work!

10 The prime minister decided to .... when she realised she had no chance of being re-elected.

11 Answer the questions below:

1 If someone **has their back against the wall**, can somebody **lend them a hand**? Why/Why not?

2 If someone needs to **cut their losses**, should they **go back to square one**? Why/Why not?

3 If someone has had a **close call**, are they **safe and sound**? Why/Why not?

4 If someone **doesn't have a hope in hell,** should they **throw in the towel**? Why/Why not?

5 Can someone be **at the end of their tether** after unsuccessfully trying to dig up their garden **with their bare hands?** Why/Why not?

12 Look at the accident scene below. Using some of the idioms from the list, discuss what might have happened.

a close call, not have a hope in hell, to sit tight, to chance it, last-ditch, to lend a hand, safe and sound, one's bare hands, in a tight corner

Unit 9

1 **Read the dialogue and try to explain the idioms in bold.**

- So Inspector ... What do you make of the burglaries?
- Well Mr Sparks, I'd say you've got **1) a rotten apple** in the company.
- Are you suggesting that staff are involved?
- That's what I said. Yes, it was certainly **2) an inside job**, masterminded by one of your own people.
- Wh-Why would you say that?
- No broken windows or locks tend to suggest that the burglar had a key. Wouldn't you agree, Mr Sparks?
- Um ...
- Come on Mr Sparks, **3) spill the beans**. We know you were involved. Just give us the details now.
- But, Inspector, I didn't do anything. Why are you **4) pointing the finger at** me?
- You thought you couldn't **5) put a foot wrong**, didn't you? But unfortunately, you and one of your accomplices were seen leaving the building.
- What rubbish! That's a lie. I was nowhere near the building!
- I'm afraid there's evidence Mr Sparks, such as the video from the security camera and the fingerprints on the safe. Hm, it appears that you didn't **6) cover your tracks** as well as you thought you had! Now ... are you going to stop lying and **7) come clean** or are you going to make it difficult for yourself?
- I never wanted to do it Inspector, but I was desperate — I needed the money. Am I going to have to **8) do time** for this?
- I'm afraid so. Yes, you're definitely **9) in hot water** Mr Sparks. Ah yes, one more thing... Are you intending to **10) carry the can** for your accomplices as well or are you going to tell me who they are?

2 **Match the items with the idioms from Ex. 1.**

a	a crime committed by sb within a company/ organisation/group, etc	**f**	to reveal information/ the truth
b	sb/sth that is a bad influence on others	**g**	to hide/get rid of incriminating evidence
c	to confess to sth	**h**	to accuse
d	in trouble	**i**	to serve a prison sentence
e	to make mistakes	**j**	to take the blame (for sb else)

3 **Fill in the gaps with phrases from the list:**

hot water, an inside job, spilt the beans, covered his tracks, puts a foot wrong

1 The criminal made sure that he had .... before he left the scene of the murder.
2 After three days of interrogation, the prisoner finally .... and told the police who his accomplice was.
3 Marjorie is very diligent and responsible in her work. She never ....
4 My sister got into .... with my parents after she stayed out late on a school night.
5 The police concluded that the crime must have been ...., as no one else but the bank employees know the combination of the safe.

4 **Fill in the gaps with phrases from the list:**

come clean, rotten apple, carry the can, point the finger at, do time

Policeman: Oliver, this is the third time in as many months I've caught you stealing. It'll probably be prison this time. What do you have to say for yourself?
Oliver: I'm sorry, Sergeant Nixon.
Policeman: It was Gary O'Grady's idea, wasn't it? He's a **1)** .... you know. Don't be a fool. Don't **2)** .... because of him. Just **3)** ....
Oliver: I won't **4)** .... my friends.
Policeman: Gary must think you're a fool, you know. You **5)** .... for him every time. Well, you'll have plenty of time to think about it in prison.

5 Read the dialogue and try to explain the idioms in bold.

— Officer Brown? It's Mrs Witherbottom from the residents' association in Widdey Grove.
— Oh yes, right. What can I do for you?
— I'm afraid we've had more break-ins, and the police don't seem to be doing anything about it. You can't just **1) brush** the problem **under the carpet**, you know!
— Mrs Witherbottom! We're doing our best!
— Oh really? Well we've been waiting for someone to **2) blow the whistle on** these burglars for long enough, so we've decided to do something about it ourselves. In fact, Mrs Simms and her dog Rambo **3) caught** one of them **red-handed** this morning!
— Mrs Simms and Rambo?
— Yes, she saw him just as he was about to break into Mrs Boyd's house, so **4) on the spur of the moment**, she set Rambo on him! Honestly, these young hooligans think they can **5) get away with murder** — **6) in broad daylight**, too!
— Oh no! Is the lad alright? I mean, you can't attack people Mrs Witherbottom — even if they are criminals! You have to do these things **7) by the book**!
— Yes, yes. Well, Rambo certainly caught him **8) off guard**! He tried to **9) cut and run**, of course, but he had no chance of escape with Rambo there!
— But is the boy okay?
— Oh yes, just a few cuts and bruises, but good old Rambo **10) taught him a lesson**, that's for sure!
— Thank goodness! Right Mrs Witherbottom, don't go anywhere. I'm on my way.

6 Match the items with the idioms from Ex. 5.

a	in the daytime/when it is easy to see	**g**	according to the law/ rules
b	to hide/ignore sth illegal/unpleasant/embarrassing, etc	**h**	to discover sb in the act of wrongdoing
c	spontaneously	**i**	to do sth terrible/illegal without being punished
d	by surprise	**j**	to stop sth bad or illegal from happening by telling the authorities
e	to punish sb in order to improve their behaviour		
f	to make a quick escape		

7 Rewrite the following sentences using the words in bold. Do not change these words in any way.

1 The Armstrongs had their house burgled in the day-time.
broad ....
2 Arthur and Vanessa suddenly decided to get married.
moment ....
3 Young Jack never gets punished because he's got such an innocent face.
murder ....
4 I'm sorry it's taking so long but we have to do it according to the law.
book ....
5 The magistrate was surprised by the reporter's comment about his alleged involvement with organised crime.
guard ....

8 Fill in the missing verbs to complete the idioms. Then, choose any three and make sentences.

1 to .... and run
2 to .... the whistle
3 to .... sb a lesson
4 to .... sth under the carpet
5 to ...... sb red-handed

9 Replace the words in bold with suitable idioms.

1 The man refused to **take all the blame** and quickly **identified** his accomplices.
2 The businessman denied having **tried to hide dishonest deals** and swore that all of his business transactions were done **legally**.
3 Unless we **get rid of the evidence**, the police are sure to find us and then we'll have to **go to prison**!
4 The police caught the thief **as he was committing the crime** so he knew he was **in big trouble**.
5 The criminal thought he could **escape without punishment** until his accomplice **told the truth** about what had happened.

10 Rewrite the following sentences using the words in bold. Do not change these words in any way.

1 When the teacher asked Mary who had stolen her book she said it was Bert.
pointed ....
2 Jill rarely makes mistakes; she's far too careful.
foot ....

3 The robber felt so guilty that he went to the police station and told them what he had done.
clean ....

4 Paul is in jail now because he stole money from the company where he worked.
time ....

5 If you lie to the police, you'll almost certainly end up in trouble.
hot ....

6 Although Sam knew he'd be expelled if he took the blame for his friends, he still wouldn't betray them.
can ....

7 The politician was ashamed of his careless mistake and tried to pretend it hadn't happened.
carpet ....

8 I know Craig read your diary — I discovered him reading it in the kitchen!
red ....

9 When Mr Simms came home the burglars managed to run away quickly.
cut ....

10 Nobody knew the truth about the actress until her ex-husband revealed her secrets in a book about their marriage.
beans ....

11 Choose the word which best completes each sentence.

1 Before they could incite the other workers, the two rotten .... were fired.
A grapes   **B** oranges   **C** apples   **D** pears

2 The detective suspected that the crime was an inside ....
A job   **B** work   **C** career   **D** task

3 The robbers didn't cover their .... very well, so the police found them easily.
A footsteps **B** rails   **C** trails   **D** tracks

4 If Marcy finds out about this, she'll soon blow the .... on what we're doing.
A whistle   **B** horn   **C** trumpet   **D** pipe

5 We decided to go to Paris for the weekend on the .... of the moment.
A spike   **B** point   **C** spur   **D** blade

6 Mrs Johnson's grandson gets away with ....; she never punishes him, no matter how naughty he is.
A assault   **B** murder   **C** robbery   **D** burglary

7 I couldn't believe it when I saw them together in .... daylight!
A thick   **B** actual   **C** full   **D** broad

8 Unless we do everything by the ...., we'll get into trouble.
A book   **B** page   **C** police   **D** law

9 The question caught the politician off .... and he fell silent, unable to find an answer.
A balance   **B** side   **C** notice   **D** guard

10 You should send him to bed without any supper. That will teach him a ....!
A subject   **B** lesson   **C** theory   **D** trick

12 Say whether the idioms in the sentences below are used correctly or incorrectly. Then replace the incorrect idioms with a suitable alternative.

1 It's going to be difficult to prove that he's guilty as he never seems to **put a foot wrong.**

2 Don't tell Greg about Jack's surprise party - he's bound to **carry the can!**

3 Most employers are unwilling to hire anyone who has **done time.**

4 The enemy caught our soldiers **off guard** and were easily able to capture the city.

5 It was amazing that no one saw the attack as it took place **in hot water.**

6 Sheila likes to plan everything carefully, so she rarely does anything **on the spur of the moment.**

7 The police rushed to the scene of the crime, but the criminals had already **blown the whistle** by the time they arrived.

8 After Bob's mother caught him pulling his sister's hair, she sent him to bed early to **catch him red-handed.**

9 The government tried to **brush the** increasing unemployment figures **under the carpet.**

10 The police were certain that the theft was a **rotten apple** as the thief had known exactly where to find the files.

13 Answer the questions below:

1 If someone **spills the beans,** do they **come clean**? Why/Why not?

2 If someone is **a rotten apple,** should you **teach them a lesson**? Why/Why not?

3 If you don't want someone **to get away with murder,** should you **blow the whistle on** them? Why/Why not?

4 If you want **to catch** someone **red-handed,** is it easier if they're **off guard**? Why/Why not?

5 If someone is **in hot water,** is it because they've **put a foot wrong**? Why/Why not?

Unit 10

1 Read the dialogue and try to explain the idioms in bold.

Mrs Brown: Hello, Miss Black, I'm Sean Brown's mother. I'd like to talk to you about how he's **1) getting to grips with** his school work. He missed so many lessons while he was in hospital ... Well, it's been hard.

Miss Black: Please sit down Mrs Brown. Yes, Sean has missed quite a bit, but I'm certain he can still **2) make the grade** if he works hard. His main weakness is in maths. At the moment, I'm afraid, he's somewhat **3) out of his depth** in the subject.

Mrs Brown: Oh, he never did **4) have a good head for figures**. He takes after me I suppose. I **5) haven't a clue** about maths either!

Miss Black: But there isn't any need to worry. As I said, I'm sure he'll be able to catch up. It just means he'll have some extra homework for a while, which I imagine he won't like! However, Sean's never been **6) slow on the uptake**, so it shouldn't be long before he **7) gets on top of** it all.

Mrs Brown: Oh, I am relieved to hear that. And, tell me, is he well-behaved in class? His father always says he could **8) talk the hind legs off a donkey!**

Miss Black: Yes. He certainly has **9) the gift of the gab**; he could even be a good politician one day! I can honestly say that Sean is a pleasure to teach. He's very polite and enthusiastic. And he **10) is head and shoulders above the rest** when it comes to English. He shows great talent in his compositions.

Mrs Brown: Well, I really have taken up enough of your time Miss Black. Thanks very much for seeing me.

Miss Black: Not at all. Goodbye!

2 Match the items with the idioms from Ex. 1.

a	to begin to understand/cope with sth, especially a problem/difficult situation	**e**	to be good at arithmetic
		f	of sb who understands and learns things slowly
b	to reach a particular standard/succeed	**g**	to talk too much
c	to deal with sth successfully	**h**	to have no knowledge of a subject
d	to be more important/greater/better than others	**i**	the talent to talk easily and persuasively
		j	unable to understand/control, especially a difficult topic/situation

3 Fill in the gaps with phrases from the list:

slow on the uptake, out of my depth, good head for figures, haven't a clue, make the grade

1 My husband has a ...., so he deals with all our money matters.
2 Steve's a bit .... It took him three weeks to realise that Sharon wasn't interested in him.
3 Teresa didn't get onto the degree course at Oxford as she didn't .... at her interview.
4 When Martin talks about computers, I'm soon .... because I have no idea how they function.
5 I've been looking for my glasses all morning; I .... where I left them.

4 Fill in the gaps with phrases from the list:

getting to grips with, talk the hind legs off a donkey, head and shoulders above, on top of, the gift of the gab

— I heard our new breakfast-show host this morning. He's brilliant — definitely **1)** .... the last one.
— I know, and he's really got **2)** .... too; you should see how much fan mail he's getting from the listeners!
— How is he **3)** .... the workload?
— Fine. He's got Mary to help him out and together they seem to be getting **4)** .... it all.
— Mary? Isn't she the one who never stops talking?
— Yes, she could **5)** ....! Actually, I was wondering if we could get her a slot on the break-fast show too ...

5 Read the letter and try to explain the idioms in bold.

Dear Giles,

I just had to write and let you know that I got the job at the law firm I was telling you about.

The interview was a bit odd because the other candidate, Mr Dalziell-Smythe, and myself, were interviewed together and I must admit I felt a bit concerned when it turned out that both he and the interviewer were **1) old boys** from Eton. Mr D.S. was a terrible snob too, and made it obvious that he thought I was **2) from the wrong side of the tracks** as soon as I mentioned that I was from Brixton. However, I needn't have worried as the **3) smart alec** soon **4) put his foot in it** when he told the interviewer that he thought the current legal system was old-fashioned and needed updating. The interviewer was clearly offended and responded by saying that being **5) of the old school** he rather admired the traditional legal ways. This comment seemed to **6) put** Mr D.S. **in his place** as he didn't say much after that.

I felt even better when I realised that Mr D.S. was **7) all at sea** as far as canon law was concerned. Fortunately, I've been studying so hard that I **8) know** the subject **inside out**, and I made sure that the interviewer knew that too!

The firm's head office called me this morning to tell me that I've been accepted and that they'd like me to go back tomorrow morning as they want me to **9) learn the ropes** as soon as possible. I'll probably ask them to tell me a bit more about the firm too, as the interviewer barely had time to **10) scratch the surface** last week.

I'll write again soon to let you know how I'm getting along.

Regards,
Craig

6 Match the items with the idioms from Ex. 5.

a to make sb understand/ admit they have done/ said sth unacceptable	f to offend/upset/ embarrass others, usually by accident
b confused	g from the poor/less respectable part of town
c former student, especially from an all-boys private school	h to know sth/sb very well
d to examine a small part of a problem/subject	i sb who thinks he/she is very clever
e old-fashioned and conservative	j to become familiar with details/methods of a job/ profession/company, etc

7 Rewrite the following sentences using the words in bold. Do not change these words in any way.

1 Roger's only just become a carpenter, so he's still developing his skills.
   ropes ....
2 My doctor is a delightful gentleman who is very traditional in his ways.
   school ....
3 Fred is always offending people; I wish he'd be more careful when he speaks.
   foot ....
4 I'm afraid your plan to slow down inflation only offers a partial solution to the problem.
   scratches..
5 Mother soon made my young cousin behave properly by giving him a good telling-off.
   place ....

8 Replace the words in bold with suitable idioms.

Don't be put off by the new accountant's appearance. He looks scruffy, as if he's **not from a respectable area**, and it can be annoying that he's **one of these people who think they know everything**, but actually he's **a former pupil** from Harrow and **he's very knowledgeable in** the field of accounting. I was **hopelessly confused** about taxes and keeping the company's books before, but now everything is in order.

9 Choose the word which best completes each sentence.

1 In order to get to .... with his divorce, Terence went for counselling.
A clasps B grips C grabs D clutches

2 I don't need a calculator, thank you. I've a good .... for figures and I'll work it out mentally.
A idea B brain C head D eye

3 If Sue wants to go to university, she'll need to work hard to make the ....
A degree B category C point D grade

4 Emma hasn't a .... about how to fix a flat tyre.
A clue B hint C sign D theory

5 Carla really has the .... of the gab; she's always the centre of attention at parties.
A blessing B bonus C present D gift

6 Anna chats so much, she could talk the .... legs off a donkey.
A back B rear C hind D left

7 Students who haven't taken the introductory course in physics will be out of their ....
A class B league C depth D head

8 If I study all weekend, I can get on .... of my maths homework.
A point B top C peak D summit

9 It took me a while to learn the .... when I started my new job.
A paths B laws C ladders D ropes

10 Bruce is a(n) .... alec — he's always telling others how to do things better.
A smart B clever C wise D intelligent

10 Fill in the gaps with phrases from the list:

head and shoulders above, inside out, slow on the uptake, old boys, scratch the surface, all at sea, putting her in her place, wrong side of the tracks, of the old school, put her foot in it

1 Sarah .... when she told Michael that he was a terrible singer.

2 I didn't understand that lesson and now I'm ....

3 It was only a short meeting so we barely had time to .... of the issue.

4 You don't find many carpenters .... any more — these days everything is done by machine.

5 Many .... turned up for the school reunion dinner.

6 Anna's a bit ....; everyone except her can see that Terry is in love with her.

7 Even though Tom was from the ...., he married Elizabeth, who was from a very rich family.

8 Mr Dark has worked here longer than any other employee so he knows the job ....

9 Catherine is .... everyone else in the basketball team — she's got a good chance of becoming the captain.

10 I don't blame Ian for ....; after all, Shirley's always criticising other people.

11 Fill in the missing verbs to complete the idioms. Then, choose any five and make sentences.

1 to .... the grade
2 to .... the surface
3 to .... a good head for figures
4 to .... the ropes
5 to .... sth inside out
6 to .... the hind legs off a donkey
7 to .... sb in their place

12 Answer the questions below:

1 Would a **smart alec** consider himself/herself to be **head and shoulders above everyone else**? Why/Why not?

2 If you were **all at sea** after your first day in a new job, would you find it easy to **get on top of** your workload? Why/Why not?

3 Would an **old boys'** reunion necessarily be a gathering of old men? Why/Why not?

4 If you feel **out of your depth** when somebody talks about a particular subject, does this mean you are **slow on the uptake**? Why/Why not?

5 If your father thought your fiancé was **from the wrong side of the tracks**, would he find it difficult to **get to grips with** your relationship? Why/Why not?

6 If you met a tailor **of the old school**, would you be surprised if he **didn't have a clue** how to sew by hand? Why/Why not?

Unit 11

1 Read the extract from a letter and try to explain the idioms in bold.

... a few months ago we decided to buy some new computers for the office as we'd had the old ones for a while and they were **1) on their last legs**. Because of the cost, however, it was something we'd been keeping **2) on the back burner** for a while. Then last month we lost a lot of valuable data because many of them were **3) on the blink**, so we agreed we couldn't postpone things any longer.

I really hadn't realised what a big job it was going to be! The old computers **4) weighed a ton** — it took two of us to carry each one downstairs — and we had to rip out all the old wiring. However, we had been thinking of rearranging the office layout for some time, so in fact, we managed to **5) kill two birds with one stone**.

We had quite a few **6) teething troubles** with the new computers, but this was mainly my fault. The company that sold them to us sent a man round to explain the **7) nuts and bolts** of the new system to me so that we could go **8) on line**. His instructions on how to operate the new computers seemed **9) as clear as a bell** when he explained everything to me, but of course, I got totally confused when trying to pass on the information to the rest of the staff! As a result, I had to ask him to come back to go through it all again — rather embarrassing I must say!

Anyway, everything's working properly now and I'm amazed at how much better they are than our old ones. I've had great fun **10) surfing the Net** and sending E-mail to everyone ...

2 Match the items with the idioms from Ex. 1.

a	to be very heavy	**g**	about to fail due to age/ exhaustion/poor health, etc
b	basic practical details		
c	to look up information on the Internet to see what is available	**h**	to fulfil two purposes with one single action
d	not working properly	**i**	into a central computer network
e	difficulties that occur in the early stages of sth		
f	postponed till a later time	**j**	very easy to hear/ understand

3 Fill in the gaps with phrases from the list:

nuts and bolts, on the blink, weighed a ton, the back burner, last legs

1 It took four people to carry the desk because it ....
2 Mr Keen explained the .... of his political campaign to supporters.
3 This typewriter is so old it hardly works. It's on its ....
4 My washing-machine's .... again - I'll have to call the repair man.
5 We'll have to put this issue on .... for the moment as we've got more pressing matters to deal with.

4 Rewrite the following sentences using the words in bold. Do not change these words in any way.

1 I had to browse for information on the Internet for hours before I finally found what I was looking for.
   surf ....
2 The library computers are connected to a central computer, so you have access to a lot of information.
   line ....
3 The construction of Wickway shopping centre had a few problems in the early stages, but they were eventually sorted out.
   teething ....
4 The instructions on the side of the fax machine were very easily understood.
   bell ....
5 I wanted to brighten up the flat and reduce the draught from the windows, so I did both at once by hanging up curtains.
   birds ....

34

5 Read the dialogue and try to explain the idioms in bold. Then, look at the picture and say which idiom it represents.

- Excuse me? I'd like to buy one of your computers, but I'm afraid I can't **1) make head or tail of** all the jargon in your catalogue.
- I know. There are so many specialized words and expressions that, for the novice, computers are quite **2) mind-boggling**, but one soon realises that a computer can **3) come in** very **handy** indeed. So, what were you planning on using your computer for, sir?
- Well, you see, I'm a writer and I've always used an old-fashioned typewriter — didn't think a computer could do the job better. For years I refused to accept their benefits but I must say I have now **4) seen the light**. To be honest I've got three new novels **5) in the pipeline**, and, well, a computer would be a great help, wouldn't it?
- Yes, you can change parts of your work easily without having to **6) go back to the drawing board** all the time.
- Mmm, that's what they say. But I'd like to see my work on paper, too.
- Ah yes, you'll be needing a printer then. There are some very good ones around today.
- So ... what should I get? I mean I don't want something that is just **7) a flash in the pan** and will be **8) past its sell-by date** in just a matter of months.
- Of course not. Now, this model here has been **9) selling like hot cakes** for two years. It's very popular, mainly because it's **10) a carbon copy** of the one sold by the leading computer company, only for half the price.

6 Match the items with the idioms from Ex. 5.

a	no longer effective/ interesting	**f**	sb/sth that is exactly the same as sb/sth else
b	popular for only a short time	**g**	to sell many of sth very quickly
c	to plan again from the beginning	**h**	to be useful
d	to understand sth/sb	**i**	in the process of being prepared/produced, etc
e	amazing or confusing	**j**	to finally understand sth after a long time

7 Fill in the missing verbs to complete the idioms. Then, choose any three and make sentences.

1 to .... head or tail of sth

2 to .... like hot cakes

3 to .... in handy

4 to .... the light

5 to .... back to the drawing board

8 Choose the word which best completes each sentence.

1 We tried to calculate the number of known stars in the universe. The number was just .... -boggling.
A head   B brain   C mind   D spirit

2 With quickly changing fashion trends these orange jumpers will soon be past their sell-by ....
A date   B season   C day   D time

3 When Sally finished sewing her wedding dress, it was a carbon .... of the one in the magazine.
A image   B duplicate   C replica   D copy

4 He attends the exhibitions every month to see what new fashions are in the ....
A grapevine   B pipeline   C oven   D tunnel

5 Ricky Rocker's stage success was just a .... in the pan — he was forgotten after six months.
A blaze   B flicker   C flash   D light

9 Rewrite the following sentences using the words in bold. Do not change the words in any way.

1 We couldn't watch the film as the television wasn't working properly.
blink ....

2 This suitcase is really heavy; what have you got in here?
ton ....

3 The engineer was concerned about the practical details of building on marshy ground.
nuts ....

4 The number of computers connected to the network is in the millions.·
line ....

5 The amount that international footballers get paid is quite amazing.
mind ....

6 Tom was totally confused by algebra until his teacher helped him to understand.
light ....

7 My holiday plans had to be postponed when several serious problems cropped up at work.
burner ....

8 Halfway through the construction of the building the architect realised that the design didn't work, so he had to start all over again.
board ....

9 Sid's car is an exact replica of the 1950s model.
carbon ....

10 A mobile phone can be very useful if you need to make an emergency phone call.
handy ....

10 Fill in the gaps with phrases from the list:

surf the Net, teething troubles, make head or tail, flash in the pan, on her last legs, in the pipeline, kill two birds with one stone, as clear as a bell, selling like hot cakes, past its sell-by date

1 I'm afraid your dog is ...., Mrs Bell; she won't live very much longer.
2 I managed to .... when I went to the post office — I bought some Christmas cards and I paid my electricity bill.
3 Sharon had a few .... when she opened her restaurant, but now business is fine.
4 Fortunately, the assembly instructions with my tent were ...., so I was able to put it up in minutes.
5 If you ...., you'll find information on just about every conceivable subject.
6 Bookshops had to order more copies of Carlos Freire's new novel as it was ....
7 Although the gadget was just a ...., the manufacturers became rich in less than a year.
8 The rock band has a new album .... and all their fans are looking forward to its release.
9 I always check the carton when I buy milk to make sure it isn't ....
10 I've read Ben's composition three times, but I still can't .... of it.

11 **Look at the two pictures. Using some of the idioms from the list, compare and contrast the two objects.**

to weigh a ton, to come in handy, to kill two birds with one stone, to surf the Net, to sell like hot cakes, to be past its sell-by date

12 **Answer the questions below:**

1 If a person had **teething troubles** in the first few weeks of setting up a new company, would they have to **go back to the drawing board**? Why/Why not?
2 If a film director explained the **nuts and bolts** of his idea for a film to a producer who thought it sounded like **a carbon copy** of another film, do you think the producer would accept the idea? Why/Why not?
3 If you couldn't **make head or tail of** a poem, would the writer be able to help you **see the light**? Why/Why not?
4 If a company has plans for a new product **in the pipeline**, does this mean that the plans have been put **on the back burner**? Why/Why not?

Unit 12

1 Read the text and try to explain the idioms in bold.

Of all the children I knew at school, the one I have the fondest memories of is Reggie Bennett. His apparent gruffness made me a bit wary of him when we first met, and I thought that he was something of **1) a rough diamond**. Through his quick wit and leadership, however, he quickly gained everyone's admiration and became the school's **2) golden boy**, both in the classroom and the playground.

Perhaps the main reason for Reggie's popularity was his ability to tell great stories about ghosts and aliens. Once, being the gullible person I am, I believed him. When I realised he'd been **3) pulling my leg** I got embarrassed, but I tried to **4) put on a brave face** so no one could tell.

Despite all the teasing, though, Reggie would never **5) stab** a friend **in the back** as, to him, disloyalty among friends was unforgivable and it really **6) made his hackles rise** if anyone talked about him **7) behind his back**. I shall never forget the time when he found out that someone had been telling everybody, untruthfully, that he had cheated in a test; Reggie got very **8) hot under the collar**.

Apart from such occasions, however, Reggie always **9) kept his cool** and thanks to his **10) down-to-earth** character, he was always the best person to consult if you needed practical advice.

I often wonder what happened to Reggie after we left school. However, I'm certain of one thing: with a character as special as his, he deserved the best in life.

2 Match the items with the idioms from Ex. 1.

a	to remain calm in a difficult situation	**f**	successful/popular person
b	a good person with uncivil/curt manners	**g**	to make sb very angry
c	realistic/practical	**h**	annoyed/frustrated/excited/worried, etc
d	to tease sb in a friendly manner	**i**	without one's knowledge/consent
e	to try to look happy/pleasant in order to hide feeling upset/embarrassed, etc	**j**	to be disloyal to a person, especially to sb who trusts one

3 Fill in the gaps with phrases from the list:

down-to-earth, stab you in the back, golden boy, put on a brave face, rough diamond

1 Mr Horner is a bit of a ....; he's got rather a harsh manner but deep down he's a very sweet man.

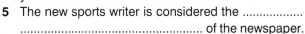

2 When I need advice I speak to Vicky because she's so sensible and ....
3 Despite losing the match we .... and congratulated the winning team.
4 Charlotte isn't a loyal friend at all. She'll be nice to your face and then ....
5 The new sports writer is considered the .... of the newspaper.

4 Fill in the gaps with phrases from the list:

hot under the collar, behind my back, makes my hackles rise, pulling your leg, keep your cool

Mary: I can't stand Ray; he truly **1)** ....!
Bob: Oh come on Mary, **2)** ....! He was only **3)** .... when he said he'd borrowed your car and crashed it. I can't understand why you're getting so **4)** ....
Mary: I'm sorry Bob, but I wouldn't be surprised if he borrowed my car **5)** .... — Ray's sly enough to do something like that!

5 Read the dialogue and try to explain the idioms in bold.

Boss: Please sit down, Peter. I understand you want to **1) get** something **off your chest**, so tell me quickly because I've got a very busy schedule this morning.

Peter: Well, sir. It's about your choice of applicant for the position of medical director, Jefferson. You know I'm not **2) a nosy Parker**, sir, but I couldn't help noticing at the interview that he was a bit of **3) a dark horse**, so I decided to do a bit of investigating.

Boss: And...?

Peter: Well, I spoke to his previous employer, a Mr Todd, and found out that he has a tendency to **4) lose his head** when faced with a difficult situation and also that he has a strong dislike of authority — apparently he has a **5) chip on his shoulder** because he's never held a senior position himself. It seems that he **6) has a** very **short fuse** as well, as he ended up hitting a patient who had disagreed with him. Of course, they fired him after that, and as Mr Todd told me, Jefferson reacted badly to that by screaming and shouting and threatening that he would **7) get his own back**! Anyway, basically I think you should offer the position to Smith instead.

Boss: Smith! But he's such **8) a wet blanket**! Don't you remember him refusing to come to last year's Christmas party because he thought it was silly?

Peter: Ah, but he's **9) as straight as a die** sir, and you know we need someone reliable for this position.

Boss: Yes, I **10) take your point**, but how are we going to give Jefferson the bad news?...

6 Match the items with the idioms from Ex. 5.

a	completely honest/fair	f	sb who is curious about other people's business
b	to accept/appreciate what sb has said	g	to have a tendency to get angry quickly/easily
c	to talk about worries/problems in order to gain relief	h	sb whose character is unknown
d	a miserable person who doesn't like others to have fun	i	sense of anger/bitterness because of unfair treatment
e	to take revenge	j	to lose control due to panic/anger, etc

7 Rewrite the following sentences using the words in bold. Do not change these words in any way.

1 Fiona never wants to do anything exciting; she's such a miserable person.
blanket ....

2 Our neighbours are such curious people, they're always peeking through their curtains to see what we're doing.
Parkers ....

3 I appreciate what you're saying, Jo, but we just can't afford a car right now.
point ....

4 Watch what you say to the director, he loses his temper very easily.
fuse ....

5 My mother became furious when my brother told her that he had been suspended from school.
lost ....

8 Choose the word which best completes each sentence.

1 Charles has had a .... on his shoulder ever since he lost the bet with Mike.
A dimple   B chip   C hole   D dent

2 Angry and upset, Harry called his sister to get a few things off his ....
A lungs   B heart   C neck   D chest

3 Bill is a bit of a dark ....; I had no idea he used to be an Olympic swimmer.
A horse   B stallion   C donkey   D steed

4 The newly-appointed Minister is as .... as a die, he's very honest and reliable.
A square   B straight   C vertical   D horizontal

5 When Tim stole my doll, I .... my own back by stealing his favourite toy car.
A retrieved   B got   C fetched   D regained

9 Fill in the gaps with phrases from the list:

nosy Parkers, stab you in the back, short fuse, rough diamond, golden boy, lost his head, wet blanket, pulling my leg, behind her back, take your point

1 Elmer may seem ungracious and blunt but in fact he's a ....

2 I thought Karen was being serious when she told me she was going to quit her job, but she was just ....

3 Whatever you do, don't trust Ken — he'll .... given half the chance.

4 Susan let Richard read her diary and then he went .... and told everyone what she had written.

5 In the '20s and '30s, Charlie Chaplin was the .... of the silver screen.

6 "Yes, yes, I .... but if we don't have any financial backing, we can't go ahead with the project."

7 As soon as Doreen came out of the director's office, all the .... wanted to know what he had wanted.

8 Excuse me, I don't mean to be a .... but I'd rather you didn't tell that joke.

9 Mr Dithers .... when his employees threatened to go on strike.

10 Although James loves children, I don't think he should become a teacher because he has such a ....

10 Rewrite the following sentences using the words in bold. Do not change these words in any way.

1 Reginald got upset when he realised that his car had a flat tyre.
collar ....

2 Even though Deborah was disappointed when her book was rejected, she hid her sadness and told her husband not to worry.
brave ....

3 Although Bob is usually an impatient man, he didn't get angry when he was stuck in traffic for an hour.
cool ....

4 Taxi drivers in this city make me mad! They're so rude and obnoxious.
hackles ....

5 Penelope is so sensible, I was stunned when she joined the circus.
earth ....

6 After Lucy's colleague stole her invention she wanted vengeance.
back ....

7 Phil has felt resentful since his schooldays because he wasn't on the football team.
shoulder ....

8 They say that the judge who is hearing this case is fair and unbiased, so you have a good chance of winning.
die ....

9 Nobody knew much about old Mr Fields as he was a secretive person, but we later found out that he was a resistance fighter during the war.
horse ....

10 It's obvious that you're worried about something so why don't you just tell me what's bothering you.
chest ....

11 Say whether the idioms in the sentences below are used correctly or incorrectly. Then replace the incorrect idioms with a suitable alternative.

1 When William wasn't accepted by any university, he **put on a brave face** and said he'd try again next year.

2 My sister is such **a dark horse** — she's always interfering in other people's business.

3 David is a bit of **a wet blanket** but, despite his gruffness, he's a very nice man.

4 Richard is always **pulling my leg;** I never know when he's being serious or not.

5 Pete Sampras is considered the **golden boy** of the tennis world. He's an outstanding player.

6 Mary got **hot under the collar** when she was told she hadn't got the promotion.

7 Alex has had **a short fuse** ever since his brother was given their father's old car.

8 In order for Arthur to **get** his problems **off his chest,** he went to see a psychologist.

9 Robert **kept his cool** when someone crashed into the back of his car because he jumped out of his car and started screaming at the other driver.

10 The behaviour of impatient drivers **takes my point.**

12 Answer the questions below:

1 Would you be surprised if a friend who was usually **as straight as a die** borrowed your favourite jacket **behind your back**? Why/Why not?

2 If you found out that somebody who you considered your friend **stabbed you in the back**, would you be tempted to **get your own back**? Why/Why not?

3 Would you expect a **down-to-earth** person to be **a dark horse**? Why/Why not?

Unit 13

1 Read the dialogue and try to explain the idioms in bold.

— Mr Whitbread, you've recently **1) come under fire** over your comments on industrial pollution. What is your response to this criticism?

— I don't regret saying what I did at all. The main obstacle to reducing pollution is still cost, so of course we need to determine who is going to **2) foot the bill**.

— Okay, Mr Whitbread, but we should act before it's too late for our planet. We will be **3) counting the cost** of this procrastination for a generation.

— I agree totally. **4) On the other hand,** what is the good of **5) breaking the bank** in an effort to guarantee ourselves a future if it's only this country that's willing to do it? I mean that would only be **6) a drop in the ocean**. To have the desired effect, every industrial nation in the world needs to contribute!

— So, what you're saying is that unless everyone else **7) toes the line**, this government won't do anything to reduce pollution levels, right?

— I don't think you need to be quite so negative, but, yes, I believe it would be very foolish for us to spend millions of pounds on a plan which we know would **8) go up in smoke**.

— Hmm... But surely we can do more than just **9) pay lip-service** to these schemes which must be carried out eventually! I mean, stricter regulation on cars for example; surely that would be **10) a step in the right direction**.

— Oh, please, now that is another matter altogether ...

2 Match the items with the idioms from Ex. 1.

a to suffer the consequences of a reckless/foolish action	**f** to voice/express agreement on sth without actually supporting it
b to be condemned/to be sharply criticised	**g** to end in nothing/to result in failure
c a very small amount compared to what is necessary/needed	**h** to leave sb without money
d to pay for sth	**i** to obey orders/rules
e however	**j** a positive action, especially towards a solution

3 Fill in the gaps with phrases from the list:

went up in smoke, a step in the right direction, on the other hand, paid lip-service, drop in the ocean

1 This car is smoother to drive than that one. That one, ..., is a bargain.
2 The price of the mansion was a mere .... compared to the multi-millionaire's staggering fortune.
3 My plans to have a quiet evening at home .... when Geoffrey arrived with six of his friends.
4 Mayor Banks lost favour with Tunstown residents as he only .... to their anxieties.
5 You really upset Janet; it would certainly be .... if you wrote and apologised to her.

4 Read the following extract from a news report and fill in the gaps with phrases from the list:

break the bank, to toe the line, counting the cost, foot the bill, came under fire

The writing is on the wall for the Chanson Group who have been given two years **1)** .... and adopt cleaner methods of production in their factories. Chanson's owners, who **2)** .... last year when it was discovered that they were releasing tons of toxic waste into the North Sea, have said that such changes will **3)** .... It seems that the Chanson Group will soon be **4)** .... of their past failure to observe regulations unless they find someone willing to help them to **5)** ....

5 Read the extract from a newspaper and try to explain the idioms in bold.

The new Environment Minister, Tony Lord, is proving himself to be **1) a breath of fresh air** in a department whose policies have proved stale and unconvincing up to now. Yesterday, he **2) was put on the spot** by the environmental group Earth SOS when he was challenged to respond to Earth SOS's latest report which has **3) brought to light** the extent of the pollution in the River Flay.

The previous Minister, Lord Garter, commissioned the Environmental Ministry to produce a special report on the River Flay last month. Based on the evidence in the report, he gave both the river and the large NFC Pharmaceuticals factory, which is situated on the river, **4) a clean bill of health**. Lord Garter reported that the environment around the factory is now **5) "as clean as a whistle"** and the water in the river is "safe enough to drink".

Earth SOS's report must have come as **6) a rude awakening** to Mr Lord since it shows that pollution in and around the river is still far above the levels permitted by law. The report refers to plantations of small trees around the NFC factory **7) burnt to a crisp** by sulphur emission, and **8) pitch-black** sediment at the bottom of the river which is the product of industrial waste. The report also notes that the previous minister is now a director of NFC Pharmaceuticals.

Mr Lord announced that the Ministry would no longer **9) bury its head in the sand** and pretend there was no problem with the River Flay and that he personally would lead a new enquiry into pollution there. He invited Earth SOS to take part. He said there was nothing to be gained by having his Ministry and environmental groups constantly **10) at loggerheads** with each other, and concluded by saying that everyone wants a cleaner and safer environment in which to live.

6 Match the items with the idioms from Ex. 5.

a to put sb in a difficult position, especially by a sudden question
b to burn sth completely
c to ignore trouble by pretending it doesn't exist
d a statement that sth/sb is in satisfactory condition/health
e in strong disagreement
f very clean
g a sudden understanding/awareness of sth unpleasant
h black/very dark
i to make known
j sb/sth refreshingly new and different

7 Rewrite the following sentences using the words in bold. Do not change these words in any way.

1 Before the General inspected their barracks, the soldiers made sure that they were very clean.
whistle ....
2 My sister and I have strongly disagreed for years — you name it, we argue about it.
loggerheads ....
3 Terry's romantic dinner was ruined when the roast in the oven caught fire.
burnt ....
4 When the lights went out, it was very dark.
black ....
5 Scarlet Snake's new record was different and exciting so everyone wanted to buy it.
fresh ....

8 Fill in the gaps with phrases from the list:

clean bill of health, brought to light, put on the spot, rude awakening, burying their heads in the sand

1 Joseph was .... when his mother demanded an explanation for his low school marks.
2 Environmental groups concerned about the issue have accused the government of ....
3 After all his aches and pains, he was relieved to be given a ....
4 We had rather a .... to the cost of phone calls when we had our first bill.
5 Residents were appalled when Cubbley Council's mismanagement of local funds was ....

9 Fill in the missing verbs to complete the idioms. Then, choose any five and make sentences.

1 to .... under fire
2 to .... the bill
3 to .... the cost
4 to .... the bank
5 to .... lip-service
6 to .... the line
7 to .... sb on the spot
8 to .... sth to a crisp
9 to .... sth to light
10 to .... up in smoke

10 Choose the word which best completes each sentence.

1 Dogs are very loyal pets. On the other ...., they can be quite noisy.
A place   **B** point   **C** foot   **D** hand

2 The school authorities agreed that implementing corporal punishment would be a .... in the right direction.
A foot   **B** step   **C** walk   **D** hop

3 The money raised at the concert was a .... in the ocean compared with the amount needed to build the new stadium.
A drop   **B** pinch   **C** spot   **D** drip

4 Michael tends to .... his head in the sand when he has problems.
A cover   **B** conceal   **C** bury   **D** hide

5 The astronauts had to be given a clean .... of health before embarking on the space mission.
A certificate **B** bill   **C** receipt **D** statement

6 The two political candidates were at .... over the new education act.
A loggerheads   **C** dispute
B odds   **D** conflict

7 The police searched the alleged murderer's flat for evidence, but it was as clean as a ....
A flute   **B** bell   **C** crystal   **D** whistle

8 It was a(n) .... awakening when John discovered he had no money in the bank.
A abrupt   **B** sudden   **C** harsh   **D** rude

9 The children were afraid to enter the cave as it was .... -black.
A pitch   **B** ebony   **C** raven   **D** darts

10 Flora's creative approach to teaching was like a .... of fresh air to her pupils.
A gasp   **B** gulp   **C** breath   **D** whiff

11 Answer the questions below:

1 If a person agrees that it's polite to **foot the bill** occasionally but never does, is he/she **paying lip-service**? Why/Why not?
2 If a person's medical record was **as clean as a whistle**, would they be given **a clean bill of health**?
3 If two friends were **at loggerheads** with each other, would their relationship **go up in smoke**? Why/ Why not?

12 Use the words missing from the sentences below to complete the crossword.

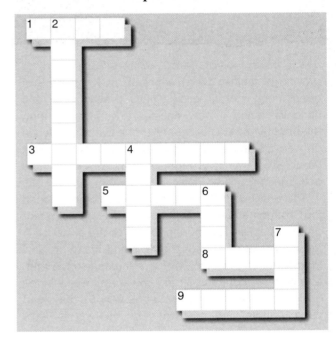

Across

1 Plans to build a new road through the village .... under fire from the council.
3 Each lesson learnt is a step in the right ....
5 The tunnel was .... -black.
8 Janet's problem was just a .... in the ocean compared to John's.
9 New evidence was brought to .... after the police investigation.

Down

2 The miners' strike in protest against their low wages was a rude .... for the Prime Minister.
4 I was burnt to a .... after lying in the sun without wearing sunblock.
6 Greg loved the author's new book; Doug, on the other ...., hated it.
7 Paul was put on the .... when his girlfriend asked him why he didn't want to marry her.

1 Read the dialogue and try to explain the idioms in bold.

— Right chaps. First of all, I'm delighted to say that our new soft drink is nearly ready to be launched. The boss told me that, as always, the name proved to be **1) a real bone of contention**. Shane Jennings wanted to call it *Fizzo* and Jennifer Biles thought *Joopy* would be a better name. Apparently they **2) went round in circles** for weeks without coming to a decision. Anyway, **3) in a nutshell**, the board of directors preferred *Joopy*, so Shane backed down when he realised he was **4) fighting a losing battle** and, consequently, it looks like it's going to be called *Joopy*. Well, you've all had several months to **5) rack your brains** for some fresh ideas, so let's **6) put our heads together** and decide on the packaging ... Sharon? Would you like to **7) start the ball rolling**?

— Hmm ...

— Okay. Frank? What about you?

— Well ...

— Come on folks! **8) Put your thinking caps on**! We don't need the precise details just yet — just **9) the bare bones** of a concept so we'll have something to start from!

— I've got it! How about a pyramid-shaped green bottle with the name in big orange letters?

— I love it!

— That's innovative! Yes, let's do that!

— Hang on! Listen you lot, the Bango Company has just used that colour scheme on their new product. We're on good terms with them and we don't want to **10) rock the boat**; they could get very upset if our packaging is too similar.

— Oh ... I see ... Let's try again then ...

2 Match the items with the idioms from Ex. 1.

a	to start a conversation/ activity, etc	**f**	to start thinking about sth, especially problem/ difficulty
b	to disturb/ruin a good situation/relation	**g**	to discuss sth, especially in order to solve a problem
c	a sensitive issue that causes argument	**h**	in few words
d	the most basic/ important parts of sth	**i**	to struggle against sth with little or no hope of success
e	to argue about the same things repeatedly without reaching a decision/solution, etc	**j**	to think hard about sth in order to find a solution/an answer

3 Fill in the gaps with phrases from the list:

started the ball rolling, bone of contention, in a nutshell, going round in circles, racked his brains

1 I won't bother going into all the details, but, ..., we have to cut down on spending costs.
2 At the company meeting, the director .... by asking if everyone was present.
3 The student .... to find the right answer to the complicated question.
4 We kept .... trying to decide what colour to paint the house but we just couldn't agree on anything.
5 Politics is a .... at home — it's a very sensitive subject as my husband's Labour and I'm Conservative.

4 Rewrite the following sentences using the words in bold. Do not change these words in any way.

1 "I don't understand you! Everything was going so well and then you had to go and spoil everything."
rock ....

2 We're way below last year's profit. I think we should meet to discuss the figures and find a way to increase our sales.
heads ....

3 The police inspector wasn't interested in details of the arrest; he just wanted to know the basics.
bare ....

4 Although the doctors tried hard to save the man, they knew his injuries were fatal.
battle ....

5 "I don't know what I'm going to do when I leave school. I guess I'll have to think about it carefully."
cap ....

5 Read the letter and try to explain the idioms in bold. Then look at the picture and say which idiom it represents.

Dear Nancy,

I thought I'd better write and explain why Pete and I won't be coming to dinner on Friday night. Basically, it's because Fred Sacks will be there and he upset Pete and me at Lisa's party last weekend.

Now, I don't know how well you're acquainted with Fred, but he always insists on **1) talking shop** on these occasions. Usually Pete and I can handle it, but he **2) got on our nerves** on Saturday when he started discussing that contract that we lost last year. Everyone knew it was Fred's fault because he'd insulted the client, but he started trying to **3) pass the buck** saying that it was Pete who'd offended her!

Well Pete does **4) not mince his words** - he told Fred to **5) get a grip** on himself and face the fact that he'd lost the contract. This clearly **6) threw** Fred **off balance** as he looked quite annoyed and embarrassed, but he still kept trying to blame Pete. I had managed to **7) hold my tongue** until then, but I couldn't stay quiet after that, so I reminded Fred of exactly how tactless he had been towards the client - I had been there at the time so he knew that I knew! Fortunately, this seemed to **8) drive home** the fact that Fred was the only one to blame, and finally he shut up!

Later on he tried to **9) clear the air** by saying that he always said stupid things when he'd had a drink, but it all **10) rang hollow**, so we ended up going home early.

Anyway, I'm sorry we can't come, but I don't want to risk having another evening like that as I'm sure you understand. Hopefully, we can get together some other time, without Fred Sacks, of course!

Love,
Anna

6 Match the items with the idioms from Ex. 5.

a	to annoy/irritate sb	**f**	to avoid responsibility/ blame by transferring it to sb else
b	to keep silent		
c	to discuss work matters when not at work	**g**	to take/maintain control (of oneself/a situation)
d	to relieve tension/ anger between people by saying/explaining sth	**h**	to confuse/surprise sb
		i	to sound false/insincere/ worthless
e	to speak frankly/ bluntly	**j**	to make sb fully aware/understand

7 Choose the word which best completes each sentence.

1 Linda told her manager that she's sick and tired of Harrison passing the .... whenever he doesn't want to take responsibility for a project.
   A buck   **B** pound   **C** bill   **D** dollar

2 That man's alibi rang .... so the police decided to find out whether or not he was lying.
   A void   **B** vacant   **C** empty   **D** hollow

3 Jim went in thinking he was well-prepared but was thrown off .... by an unexpected line of questioning.
   A symmetry **B** level   **C** balance   **D** evenness

4 I've warned Harold that he mustn't talk .... at home.
   A store   **B** shop   **C** company **D** business

5 Betty gets on my .... when she talks about her doll collection.
   A toes   **B** nerves   **C** shoulders **D** brain

8 Fill in the missing verbs to complete the idioms. Then, choose any three and make sentences.

1 to .... one's tongue
2 to .... the air
3 not to .... one's words
4 to .... home
5 to .... a grip

9 Rewrite the following sentences using the words in bold. Do not change these words in any way.

1 "I know you lost that folder; don't try to blame anyone else!"
   buck ....

44

2 The boy's excuse for missing school sounded unconvincing, so the headmaster called his parents.
rang ....

3 The detective's question confused the suspect and he started to look around nervously.
threw ....

4 "Do you mind if we discuss business for a minute?"
shop ....

5 People who use mobile phones on trains really irritate me!
nerves ....

6 The boy kept quiet while the teacher explained even though he knew the answer.
tongue ....

7 "How was my holiday? Well, to put it concisely, it was awful!"
nutshell ....

8 Tim thought hard, but he still couldn't remember the woman's name.
brains ....

9 On their first date, Phil started the conversation by asking her what her father did for a living.
ball ....

10 After their argument Tom bought his wife some flowers in an attempt to get rid of any bad feelings.
clear ....

10 Fill in the gaps with phrases from the list:

going round in circles, bone of contention, put our heads together, rock the boat, put their thinking caps on, drove home, get a grip, mince his words, fighting a losing battle, the bare bones

1 Graham is so annoying; he always tries to .... and cause trouble when we have meetings.

2 The lawyer didn't ...., and told Charlie that he would almost certainly lose the case.

3 The President's live national broadcast .... the fact that the threat of war was serious.

4 I think we should .... and think of a special present for Mum's sixtieth birthday.

5 Mr Morley's secretary told him only .... of the issues discussed at the meeting.

6 We're just .... now — I think we should go and ask Bill to help us come to a decision.

7 The police chief told his officers to .... on the situation and stop the riots.

8 The naming of the new baby proved to be a .... between her parents.

9 The protesters seem to be .... in their attempts to halt the extension of Langley Road.

10 The teacher told the students to .... and solve the mathematical problem.

11 Say whether the idioms in the sentences below are used correctly or incorrectly. Then replace the incorrect idioms with a suitable alternative.

1 Carl is forever trying to **talk shop** — he never takes responsibility for his mistakes.

2 The advertising executives **racked their brains** trying to come up with a promotional campaign.

3 At the press conference, one of the reporters **held his tongue** and asked the first question.

4 Pocket money is **the bare bones** in our house; the subject starts huge arguments whenever it is brought up.

5 The Minister's speech **rang hollow** — no one believed a word he said.

6 My father does **not mince his words** — he always gets straight to the point.

7 John's proposal of marriage **drove me home** and I didn't know how to reply.

8 It will take too long to explain everything in detail, but **in a nutshell**, we're going to have to make redundancies.

9 Why does Peter insist on **rocking the boat** all the time? Why can't he just let things be?

10 George told Mary to **clear the air** and stop crying.

12 Answer the questions below:

1 Does it **get on your nerves** when you find yourself in an argument and you're just **going round in circles**? Why/Why not?

2 If you were in a meeting and your boss suggested everyone **put their heads together** to find a solution to a problem, would it help if you **put your thinking caps on**? Why/Why not?

3 Are you more or less likely to get what you want when you're **fighting a losing battle**? Why/Why not?

1 Read the dialogue and try to explain the idioms in bold.

— Well, I'm not **1) taking it lying down**! The management's proposal to increase our working hours without increasing our pay is unacceptable. We must protest. We've got to do something about it!

— Oh, don't worry. I'm sure they'll back down. The management's full of **2) hot air** — they never do what they say they're going to do.

— No, no, I believe they're serious and we can't let that happen. I think we've got to **3) dig our heels in** over this one, and I reckon most of the staff will feel the same.

— Just a minute! **4) Taking the law into your own hands** is not a solution. Organising something like that could **5) seal your fate** in this company. You could lose your job.

— No, I'm **6) sticking to my guns**. We've got to do something radical — we've been quiet for too long. It's people like you who **7) sit on the fence** that encourage management to treat us with no respect.

— I'm **8) up in arms** about the proposal too! But can't we talk the management round to our point of view? I reckon we could explain that the workforce will **9) vote with their feet** and get jobs elsewhere —that should **10) do the trick**.

2 Match the items with the idioms from Ex. 1.

a	to ensure the death/ failure of sth/sb	**f**	angry because one is opposed to sth
b	to accept sth harmful/ unpleasant without complaint/a struggle	**g**	to show one's opinion by (not) participating in sth/(not) going somewhere
c	false promises/claims	**h**	to keep supporting a particular belief/ course of action, etc
d	to do sth to combat injustice without abiding by the rules/law	**i**	to show firmness over sth, especially one's own desires
e	to refuse to have an opinion or take sides on an issue	**j**	to achieve what is wanted

3 Fill in the gaps with phrases from the list:

sealed his fate, hot air, voting with their feet, the law into their own hands, stuck to his guns

1 Ralph is so full of .... that I never take what he says seriously.

2 When the mob take .... the outcome is disastrous.

3 Although he was heavily criticised, the Minister ....

4 Hastings .... when he contradicted his boss in public.

5 By .... and opening on Sundays shopkeepers were able to change the law on opening hours.

4 Rewrite the following sentences using the words in bold. Do not change these words in any way.

1 My mother is not someone who takes poor service without complaint.
lying ....

2 Citizens are furious over the council's decision to knock down the old library.
arms ....

3 The little boy was adamant and refused to go to summer camp.
heels ....

4 Changing the spark plugs should sort it out; the car will start more easily.
trick ....

5 If Barker's Butchers don't improve the quality of their meat, housewives will show their preference by shopping at Phipp's.
feet ....

5 Read the two newspaper reports and try to explain the idioms in bold.

A The **1) running battle** between the Union of Teachers and the government over wages intensified on Tuesday after Union leader, Gerry Tuffnal, threatened strike action unless teachers are granted a 5% pay rise.

The Minister of Education, Stanley Baxter, announced yesterday that giving a rise was **2) easier said than done** as it would mean increasing taxes. However, his words seemed to **3) fall on deaf ears** as **4) the grass roots** of the Union were still in support of strike action yesterday afternoon.

Stanley Baxter and Gerry Tuffnal are currently holding discussions together **5) behind closed doors** in an attempt to come to some kind of compromise.

B Protesters are continuing to obstruct construction work on the proposed site for Stackton Airport's new runway in spite of police threats to remove them by force unless they **6) call it a day**.

Yesterday afternoon the ringleader, known only as "Josh", announced that the threats were **7) cutting no ice** with him and his colleagues. He added that if force were to be used on the demonstrators, who had been peaceful so far, **8) the law of the jungle** would apply thereafter. He also quoted **9) chapter and verse** an agreement not to extend the airport, signed by airport officials and the Minister of Transport in 1986.

The current Transport Minister, Jack Glenn retaliated last night saying that the protesters had no right to **10) sit in judgement** as the Ministry of the Environment had since granted permission for a new runway on the site. He ended his statement saying that arrests would be made if the protest were to become disorderly.

6 Match the items with the idioms from Ex. 5.

a	sth which sounds/ appears simple but is difficult to achieve/do	g	to decide if sb/sth is good or bad
b	ordinary people, not in authority but whose opinions are influential	h	the situation where the law is disregarded and the strongest/most aggressive succeed
c	long-lasting struggle	i	to stop doing sth
d	in private/secretly	j	to be ignored, especially of speech/advice
e	to fail to impress		
f	in full detail		

7 Rewrite the following sentences using the words in bold. Do not change these words in any way.

1 Demands for change are coming from the supporters of the Labour Party.
   roots ....

2 It is not for me to pass comment; Platt doesn't work for me.
   sit ....

3 Giving up smoking sounds simple but it is very difficult.
   easier ....

4 Before I tackle the Home Office, I'll need the full details on this case.
   chapter ....

5 There has been an ongoing argument between port authorities and fishermen over fishing zones.
   battle ....

8 Fill in the gaps with phrases from the list:

call it a day, law of the jungle, behind closed doors, deaf ears, cuts no ice

1 Our complaints to the Collins about their barking dog have fallen on ....

2 Her show of sincerity .... with me. I know she's lying.

3 Jury decisions are made .... to ensure the privacy of jury members while reaching their verdict.

4 After working for fifteen hours, Peter decided to .... and go home.

5 It was the .... during the January sales; bargain hunters fought to be the first to snap up the goods.

9 **Choose the word which best completes each sentence.**

1 The activists' protest against the extension of the power station fell on .... ears.
A closed   **B** deaf   **C** mute   **D** numb

2 I'm afraid Chris' witty comments .... no ice with me.
A thaw   **B** freeze   **C** melt   **D** cut

3 After failing her law exam for the third time, Jessica decided to .... it a day.
A call   **B** declare   **C** announce   **D** consider

4 The meeting was for the partners only and was held behind .... doors.
A fastened   **B** bolted   **C** closed   **D** locked

5 Your computer works fine now. I just reloaded the programme and that did the ....
A joke   **B** trick   **C** work   **D** good

6 The grass .... of the party have been demanding improvements in education for years.
A cores   **B** bases   **C** foundations   **D** roots

7 The medical profession .... with their feet by refusing to prescribe Pomvol.
A voted   **B** decided   **C** elected   **D** returned

8 Detective Armstrong wanted to be given .... and verse on the backgrounds of murder victims.
A page   **B** chapter   **C** poem   **D** section

9 "How can you sit in .... over the exhibition when you know nothing about art?"
A discrimination   **B** understanding   **C** judgement   **D** punishment

10 Following the fall of dictatorships, often it is the .... of the jungle which rules.
A code   **B** rule   **C** regulation   **D** law

10 **Fill in the gaps with phrases from the list:**

hot air, stick to our guns, running battle, take the law into their own hands, up in arms

- Sir, we must do something about this **1)** .... with the townspeople over the new car park. They're **2)** .... over the plan and I'm a bit worried that things might get nasty!
- Oh, come on, Cotter! All this talk of action is just a load of **3)** ....!
- But sir! What if they **4)** ....? They might attempt to use their own methods to get ...
- They won't go that far! Look, all we need to do is **5)** .... and they'll soon calm down!

11 **Fill in the gaps with phrases from the list:**

sealed their fates, dug his heels in, sitting on the fence, easier said than done, take these plans lying down

- Mrs Jackson, the Mayor has really **1)** .... on the subject of the new car park. I suggest that we hold a demonstration!
- Now, Mr Tyke, you know that's **2)** .... — most of the residents are pensioners and, well, they're just not up to marches!
- But they're not going to **3)** .... either!
- Relax Mr Tyke. Listen, we've got Councillor Cotter who seems to be just **4)** .... and refusing to say publicly whether or not he approves of the plans, and the Mayor who's simply ignoring the demands of those who put him where he is today. Basically, they've both **5)** ....; they'll be out of a job next year, so all we've got to do is keep stalling their plans till then.

12 **Using some of the idioms from the list discuss a) why you think the people below are protesting and, b) what consequences the demonstration might have.**

the grass roots, to take sth lying down, behind closed doors, to fall on deaf ears, to take the law into one's own hands, up in arms, to vote with one's feet, to stick to one's guns, to dig one's heels in, the law of the jungle, to call it a day, to do the trick

Glossary

Glossary

Unit 1

1.1 **down in the dumps** = depressed

1.2 **keep sb in the dark** = to keep sb unaware of sth

1.3 **not be all it/he/she/you, etc is cracked up to be** = to be not as good as people say

1.4 **catch sb's eye** = to get sb's attention

1.5 **right up one's street** = within one's range of interests/knowledge

1.6 **take things easy** = to relax

1.7 **off the beaten track** = isolated and quiet

1.8 **come down to earth with a bump** = to stop dreaming and start thinking practically

1.9 **in one's element** = very happy/suited to a situation

1.10 **the crack of dawn** = very early in the morning

1.11 **get away from it all** = to take a break from work or problems

1.12 **run-of-the-mill** = ordinary and unexciting

1.13 **as brown as a berry** = very suntanned

1.14 **round-the-clock** = all day and all night

1.15 **one's best bet** = the most appropriate choice

1.16 **over the moon** = extremely pleased

1.17 **get into the swing of sth** = to become accustomed to sth and start enjoying it

1.18 **steer clear (of sb/sth)** = to avoid (sb/sth)

1.19 **let one's hair down** = to relax and enjoy oneself

1.20 **a new lease of life** = a return of energy or enthusiasm

Unit 2

2.1 **an old flame** = sb one was once in love with

2.2 **steal sb's heart** = to make sb fall in love with one

2.3 **the man of one's dreams** = the ideal man (**Note: the woman of one's dreams** = the ideal woman)

2.4 **(be/fall) head over heels in love** = (to be/become) very much in love with sb

2.5 **break sb's heart** = to cause sb great unhappiness

2.6 **a change of heart** = a change of one's feelings for sth/sb

2.7 **wear one's heart on one's sleeve** = to allow one's feelings to be too obvious

2.8 **see eye to eye** = to agree (about matters)

2.9 **all's fair in love and war** = all actions are justified when there are feelings of love/rivalry

2.10 **be the bee's knees** = to be the best there is

2.11 **donkey's years** = a long time

2.12 **bury the hatchet** = to forget old quarrels

2.13 **the apple of sb's eye** = sb one is most fond of

2.14 **the black sheep of the family** = a person strongly disapproved of by members of his/her family

2.15 **play hard to get** = to pretend one is not interested in sb

2.16 **like putty in sb's hands** = easily controlled or manipulated

2.17 **drive sb round the bend** = to annoy sb a lot

2.18 **tie the knot** = to get married

2.19 **in clover** = in comfort/wealth

2.20 **blood is thicker than water** = blood ties or family relationships are the strongest

Unit 3

3.1 **give sb the boot** = to fire sb from their job

3.2 **a lame duck** = a person/company that is weak/a failure

3.3 **feel the pinch** = to suffer because of lack of money

3.4 **in the red** = in debt

3.5 **hit rock bottom** = to reach the lowest point

3.6 **in the black** = in credit/making profit

3.7 **play with fire** = to take dangerous risks

3.8 **step into sb's shoes** = to replace sb

3.9 **a firm hand** = control and discipline

3.10 **pay dividends** = to bring advantages at a later date

3.11 **a small fortune** = a lot of money

3.12 **mean business** = to be serious about what one says/intends

3.13 **get sth off the ground** = to start a business/company/project, etc

3.14 **bear fruit** = to produce good results

3.15 **live on a shoestring** = to manage with very little money

3.16 **burn the midnight oil** = to work very late at night to achieve sth

3.17 **be rolling in it** = to be rich

3.18 **keep one's head above water** = to survive despite financial problems

3.19 **money down the drain** = money wasted

3.20 **tighten one's belt** = to live on a smaller budget

Unit 4

4.1 **food for thought** = sth to think about

4.2 **whet one's appetite** = to make sb keen to experience/taste more of sth

4.3 **at a loss for words** = unable to think of anything to say

4.4 **make one's mouth water** = to cause sb to desire sth, especially food

4.5 **cut corners** = to use a cheaper/easier method

4.6 **in full swing** = at a very lively stage/point

4.7 **pull a few strings** = to use influence to achieve sth

Glossary

4.8 **cannot hold a candle to sb/sth** = cannot be compared favourably with sb/sth

4.9 **pick up the tab** = to pay for sth

4.10 **feast one's eyes on sb/sth** = to look with pleasure at sth/sb

4.11 **not be one's cup of tea** = not to be to one's taste

4.12 **scrape the bottom of the barrel** = to be left with/use the worst person/object

4.13 **break the ice** = to make sb relax/to get conversation started

4.14 **in the soup** = in trouble

4.15 **turn sb's stomach** = to cause sb to feel sick/ disgusted

4.16 **cast pearls before swine** = to offer sth good to sb who cannot appreciate the value of it

4.17 **it's no use crying over spilt milk** = there is no point in regretting sth that has happened

4.18 **sour grapes** = negative attitude/bitterness because of jealousy

4.19 **as dry as a bone** = very dry

4.20 **up to scratch** = of the desired standard

Unit 5

5.1 **take sth with a pinch of salt** = to doubt/consider sth untrue

5.2 **at death's door** = about to die

5.3 **off colour** = unwell

5.4 **full of beans** = very lively and energetic

5.5 **go downhill** = to get worse in health/quality/status, etc

5.6 **nothing but skin and bone** = very thin

5.7 **a shadow of one's former self** = weaker or less capable than one used to be

5.8 **up and about** = active after an illness

5.9 **as strong as an ox** = very strong and fit

5.10 **ripe old age** = very old age

5.11 **kick the bucket** = to die

5.12 **alive and kicking** = still alive and active

5.13 **touch and go** = uncertain

5.14 **the writing is on the wall** = a sign/warning of danger/unhappiness/failure, etc

5.15 **hold one's own** = to manage despite difficulties/ obstacles

5.16 **grin from ear to ear** = to smile broadly

5.17 **there's life in the old dog yet** = one is still physically/mentally energetic despite old age

5.18 **as blind as a bat** = blind or unable to see well

5.19 **have (got) one foot in the grave** = to be near death

5.20 **run out of steam** = to lose the energy that one had previously

Unit 6

6.1 **the top of the ladder** = the highest position in one's profession

6.2 **down-and-out** = person with no job or home

6.3 **live rough** = to live under unpleasant conditions

6.4 **as poor as a church mouse** = extremely poor

6.5 **from rags to riches** = from being very poor to being very rich

6.6 **up-and-coming** = likely to become successful

6.7 **right hand man** = close and trusted assistant

6.8 **call the shots** = to make the important decisions

6.9 **the jet set** = group of rich and fashionable people who are interested in enjoyment

6.10 **the slippery slope** = sth that is difficult to stop once it has begun and which usually ends badly

6.11 **have (got) several irons in the fire** = to have several options/projects at the same time

6.12 **at full stretch** = using all one's energy to do sth

6.13 **a dead end** = sth which leads nowhere and has no future

6.14 **adopt a low profile** = to avoid public attention

6.15 **take a back seat** = to take a position of less importance/influence

6.16 **the rat race** = the struggle for success, especially in a large city

6.17 **(the) big guns** = important and powerful people

6.18 **have time on one's hands** = to have spare time

6.19 **do one's own thing** = to do whatever one wants

6.20 **keep up with the Joneses** = to be in competition with other people for a higher social standard

Unit 7

7.1 **break the mould** = to completely change the way sth is done

7.2 **all the rage** = very popular/fashionable

7.3 **(just) around the corner** = very close in time/distance

7.4 **break new ground** = to develop sth/to make innovations

7.5 **old hat** = old-fashioned

7.6 **the last word** = the best/most recent version of sth

7.7 **state-of-the-art** = using the most modern techniques

7.8 **streets ahead** = more advanced

7.9 **on the horizon** = expected/likely to happen soon

7.10 **from scratch** = from the beginning and without any help

7.11 **past it** = too old to work well or safely

7.12 **stand the test of time** = to prove reliable/valuable over a long period

7.13 **in one's day** = at a time in the past when sb was young/popular/successful, etc

7.14 **live in the past** = to behave as if what existed in the past still exists

7.15 **as old as the hills** = very old

7.16 **brand new** = completely new

7.17 **turn the clock back** = to go back in time, especially to sth now considered old-fashioned

7.18 **up-to-date** = modern/new

7.19 **move with the times** = to progress with changing customs/fashions, etc

7.20 **till the cows come home** = for a long time

Unit 8

8.1 **last-ditch** = final (attempt/effort, etc)

8.2 **cut one's losses** = to give up doing sth so as to limit/ prevent further loss/damage

8.3 **the tip of the iceberg** = the tiniest sign of a larger problem

8.4 **vanish into thin air** = to disappear completely

8.5 **out of hand** = out of control

8.6 **not have a hope in hell** = to have no chance

8.7 **lend a hand** = to help

8.8 **sit tight** = not to change one's position/to stay where one is

8.9 **close call** = a close encounter with danger

8.10 **chance it** = to take a risk

8.11 **pick up the pieces** = to restore a situation after confusion/disaster

8.12 **back to square one** = back to the beginning

8.13 **by the skin of one's teeth** = only just

8.14 **with one's bare hands** = without tools/machinery, etc

8.15 **safe and sound** = safe and uninjured

8.16 **in a tight corner** = in a difficult/awkward situation

8.17 **deliver the goods** = to produce the promised/ expected results

8.18 **have one's back against the wall** = to be in a desperate situation in which one must struggle to survive

8.19 **at the end of one's tether** = at the point of losing one's patience

8.20 **throw in the towel** = to give up

Unit 9

9.1 **a rotten apple** = sb/sth that is a bad influence on others

9.2 **an inside job** = a crime committed by sb within a company/organisation/group, etc

9.3 **spill the beans** = to reveal information/the truth

9.4 **point the finger at** = to accuse

9.5 **put a foot wrong** = to make mistakes

9.6 **cover one's tracks** = to hide/get rid of incriminating evidence

9.7 **come clean** = to confess to sth

9.8 **do time** = to serve a prison sentence

9.9 **in hot water** = in trouble

9.10 **carry the can** = to take the blame (for sb else)

9.11 **brush sth under the carpet** = to hide/ignore sth illegal/unpleasant/embarrassing, etc

9.12 **blow the whistle on** = to stop sth bad or illegal from happening by telling the authorities

9.13 **catch sb red-handed** = to discover sb in the act of wrongdoing

9.14 **on the spur of the moment** = spontaneously

9.15 **get away with murder** = to do sth terrible/illegal without being punished

9.16 **in broad daylight** = in the daytime/when it is easy to see

9.17 **by the book** = according to the law/rules

9.18 **off guard** = by surprise

9.19 **cut and run** = to make a quick escape

9.20 **teach sb a lesson** = to punish sb in order to improve their behaviour

Unit 10

10.1 **get to grips with sth** = to begin to understand/cope with sth, especially a problem/difficult situation

10.2 **make the grade** = to reach a particular standard/to succeed

10.3 **out of one's depth** = unable to understand/control, especially a difficult topic/situation

10.4 **have a (good) head for figures** = to be good at arithmetic

10.5 **not have a clue** = to have no knowledge of a subject

10.6 **slow on the uptake** = of sb who understands and learns things slowly

10.7 **get on top of sth** (also: **be on top of sth**) = to deal with sth successfully

10.8 **talk the hind legs off a donkey** = to talk too much

10.9 **the gift of the gab** = the talent to talk easily and persuasively

10.10 **be head and shoulders above the rest** = to be more important/greater/better than others

10.11 **old boy** = former student, especially from an all-boys private school (**Note: old girl** when referring to students from all-girls schools)

10.12 **from the wrong side of the tracks** = from the poor/less respectable part of town

10.13 **smart alec** = sb who thinks he/she is very clever

10.14 **put one's foot in it** = to offend/upset/embarrass others, usually by accident

10.15 **of the old school** = old-fashioned and conservative

10.16 **put sb in their place** = to make sb understand/admit they have done/said sth unacceptable

10.17 **all at sea** = confused

10.18 **know sth/sb inside out** = to know sth/sb very well

10.19 **learn the ropes** = to become familiar with details /methods of a job/profession/company, etc

10.20 **scratch the surface** = to examine a small part of a problem/subject

Unit 11

11.1 **on sb's/sth's last legs** = about to fail due to age/exhaustion/poor health, etc

11.2 **on the back burner** = postponed till a later time

11.3 **on the blink** = not working properly

11.4 **weigh a ton** = to be very heavy

11.5 **kill two birds with one stone** = to fulfil two purposes with one single action

11.6 **teething troubles** = difficulties that occur in the early stages of sth

11.7 **nuts and bolts** = basic practical details

11.8 **on line** = into a central computer network

11.9 **as clear as a bell** = very easy to hear/understand

11.10 **surf the Net** = to look up information on the Internet to see what is available

11.11 **make head or tail of** = to understand

11.12 **mind-boggling** = amazing or confusing

11.13 **come in handy** = to be useful

11.14 **see the light** = to finally understand sth after a long time

11.15 **in the pipeline** = in the process of being prepared/produced, etc

11.16 **go back to the drawing board** = to plan again from the beginning

11.17 **a flash in the pan** = popular for only a short time

11.18 **past sb's/sth's sell-by date** = no longer effective/interesting

11.19 **sell like hot cakes** = to sell many of sth very quickly

11.20 **a carbon copy** = sb/sth that is exactly the same as sb/sth else

Unit 12

12.1 **a rough diamond** = a good person with uncivil/curt manners

12.2 **golden boy** = successful/popular person

12.3 **pull sb's leg** = to tease sb in a friendly manner

12.4 **put on a brave face** = to try to look happy/pleasant in order to hide feeling upset/embarrassed, etc

12.5 **stab sb in the back** = to be disloyal to a person, especially to sb who trusts one

12.6 **make sb's hackles rise** = to make sb very angry

12.7 **behind one's back** = without one's knowledge/consent

12.8 **hot under the collar** = annoyed/frustrated/excited/worried, etc

12.9 **keep one's cool** = to remain calm in a difficult situation

12.10 **down-to-earth** = realistic/practical

12.11 **get sth off one's chest** = to talk about worries/problems in order to gain relief

12.12 **a nosy Parker** = sb who is curious about other people's business

12.13 **a dark horse** = sb whose character is unknown

12.14 **lose one's head** = to lose control due to panic/anger, etc

12.15 **chip on one's shoulder** = sense of anger/bitterness because of unfair treatment

12.16 **have a short fuse** = to have a tendency to get angry quickly/easily

12.17 **get one's own back** = to take revenge

12.18 **a wet blanket** = a miserable person who doesn't like others to have fun

12.19 **as straight as a die** = completely honest/fair

12.20 **take sb's point** = to accept/appreciate what sb has said

Unit 13

13.1 **come under fire** = to be condemned/to be sharply criticised

13.2 **foot the bill** = to pay for sth

13.3 **count the cost** = to suffer the consequences of a reckless/foolish action

13.4 **on the other hand** = however

13.5 **break the bank** = to leave sb without money

13.6 **a drop in the ocean** = a very small amount compared to what is necessary/needed

13.7 **toe the line** = to obey orders/rules

13.8 **go up in smoke** = to end in nothing/to result in failure

13.9 **pay lip-service** = to voice/express agreement on sth without actually supporting it

13.10 **a step in the right direction** = a positive action, especially towards a solution

13.11 **a breath of fresh air** = sb/sth refreshingly new and different

13.12 **put sb on the spot** = to put sb in a difficult position, especially by a sudden question

13.13 **bring to light** = to make known

13.14 **a clean bill of health** = statement that sth/sb is in satisfactory condition/health

13.15 **as clean as a whistle** = very clean

13.16 **a rude awakening** = a sudden understanding/awareness of sth unpleasant

13.17 **burn to a crisp** = to burn completely

13.18 **pitch-black** = black/very dark

13.19 **bury one's head in the sand** = to ignore trouble by pretending it doesn't exist.

13.20 **at loggerheads (with sb)** = in strong disagreement

Unit 14

14.1 **a bone of contention** = a sensitive issue that causes argument

14.2 **go round in circles** = to argue about the same things repeatedly without reaching a decision/solution, etc

14.3 **in a nutshell** = in few words

14.4 **fight a losing battle** = to struggle against sth with little or no hope of success

14.5 **rack one's brains** = to think hard about sth in order to find a solution/an answer

14.6 **put our/your, etc heads together** = to discuss sth, especially in order to solve a problem

14.7 **start the ball rolling** = to start a conversation/activity, etc

14.8 **put one's thinking cap on** = to start thinking about sth, especially a problem/difficulty

14.9 **the bare bones** = the most basic/important parts of sth

14.10 **rock the boat** = to disturb/ruin a good situation/relation

14.11 **talk shop** = to discuss work matters when not at work

14.12 **get on one's nerves** = to annoy/irritate sb

14.13 **pass the buck** = to avoid responsibility/blame by transferring it to sb else

14.14 **not mince one's words** = to speak frankly/bluntly

14.15 **get a grip** = to take/maintain control (of oneself/a situation)

14.16 **throw sb off balance** = to confuse/surprise sb

14.17 **hold one's tongue** = to keep silent

14.18 **drive home** = to make sb fully aware/understand

14.19 **clear the air** = to relieve tension/anger between people by saying/explaining sth

14.20 **ring hollow** = to sound false/insincere/worthless

Unit 15

15.1 **take sth lying down** = to accept sth harmful/unpleasant without complaint/a struggle

15.2 **hot air** = false promises/claims

15.3 **dig one's heels in** = to show firmness over sth, especially one's own desires

15.4 **take the law into one's own hands** = to do sth to combat injustice without abiding by the rules/law

15.5 **seal sb's/sth's fate** = to ensure the death/failure of sth/sb

15.6 **stick to one's guns** = to keep supporting a particular belief/course of action, etc

15.7 **sit on the fence** = to refuse to have an opinion or take sides on an issue

15.8 **up in arms** = angry because one is opposed to sth

15.9 **vote with one's feet** = to show one's opinion by (not) participating in sth/(not) going somewhere

15.10 **do the trick** = to achieve what is wanted

15.11 **running battle** = long-lasting struggle

15.12 **easier said than done** = sth which sounds/appears simple but is difficult to achieve/do

15.13 **fall on deaf ears** = to be ignored, especially of speech/advice

15.14 **the grass roots** = ordinary people, not in authority but whose opinions are influential

15.15 **behind closed doors** = in private/secretly

15.16 **call it a day** = to stop doing sth

15.17 **cut no ice** = to fail to impress

15.18 **the law of the jungle** = the situation where the law is disregarded and the strongest/most aggressive succeed

15.19 **chapter and verse** = in full detail

15.20 **sit in judgement** = to decide if sb/sth is good or bad